SH*T
CREEK
TO
SOMEWHERE
ELSE

SH*T CREEK

CREEK

TO

SOMEWHERE ELSE

The options to change
even when all the odds
are against you

ANGIE CLARKE

Rethink

First published in Great Britain in 2021 by Rethink Press (www.rethinkpress.com)

© Copyright Angie Clarke

ISBN 978-1-78133-611-3

Cover image © Shutterstock | SvetaZi

Contents

Preface

We all have memories that affect us and how we are today, but we also have opportunities to make choices and build resilience. I came to a point in my life where more and more people around me were suggesting that I write about my memories; I would like to have read a book like this when I was on my own journey of change, and so I did just that. If it only helps one person, it will have been worthwhile. Everything in this book is my truth, not anyone else's, and the facts are what *I* remember, no one else. I appreciate that it might not be easy reading, but it's an honest reflection of my memory bank at the time of writing. I have changed some details to protect the anonymity of individuals.

Personally, I have really enjoyed this journey, and I am already planning my second and third books.

Thank you for buying this, my first book, and taking the time to read it. I hope it will help you in some way. If it doesn't, then feel free to pass it on to a friend or a charity shop. You never know – there may be someone else out there who will turn their life around after reading it.

Introduction

Sitting in Orange Corner, a café-bar that looks out on to the beach in St Antonio on Ibiza, I felt that it was time – time to share my knowledge. Orange Corner is my favourite place to people-watch. I have spent many happy times hanging out there with my family, sharing food, dancing, sheltering from torrential rain and enjoying the views when the weather is clear. The staff and owners are friendly and welcoming, the food is good value – if you are ever visiting the area, I encourage you to pop in to meet the team.

Now you know where my writing journey began, I would like to share a little bit of background as to why I have written this book. Quite simply, I have always wanted to share my journey and what I have learned throughout the years, am learning and continue to learn about how to lead a successful, happy life with a beautiful family and friends.

Why should you read this book? I hope it will inspire you. Anyone can change if they want to, but change isn't always the way forward. Sometimes, believing and trusting in yourself can be enough.

I didn't have much luck in my early days, but as time has gone on, I have fulfilled many of my hopes and dreams. There are some still to come, some that have been realised through others and some that I've let go of. It's fine to change your mind.

None of this would have been possible without my husband, kids and friends, as well as the professionals. You can't always get through life on your own, so why make it hard on yourself when sharing the load can lighten it? But the people you rely on to help you have to be the right ones, not the wrong ones, and sometimes telling the difference can be difficult.

My story has ups and downs, tears and laughter, and takes some unexpected avenues. Hang in there and enjoy the journey alongside me.

ONE
Choices

We all make choices, but we don't always get them right. But sometimes, even the wrong choice can serve us well. In this chapter, I'm going to look at my journey through the lens of some of the life choices I have made.

I am currently reading a book about, to put it bluntly, getting your shit together. This has triggered many memories of times and places when I have done just that, sometimes reluctantly, knowing if I didn't change then, that would be that. Everything would stay the same and I would get the same outcomes I had done in my past.

Changing is not always the easy path to follow, but it's an option that we all have. Is it an option we should always take? Some changes lead to improvements, some don't; some will alter our lives for the better, some won't, so always start the journey with a map of where you want to go, when you would like to arrive and who you want to take with you. Then the chances of having to make diversions, meeting roadworks, observing the odd accident and hoping that no one was seriously hurt are significantly diminished. Moaning and groaning about things that are out of our control gets us nowhere; we need to accept them and move on with our journey.

If life was easy, would we really appreciate the good times? Or would it all become just one continual experience with nothing against which to make a comparison? Is it true that whatever doesn't kill you makes you stronger? Only you can decide that for yourself. Who am I to decide for you? I am just happy to have the opportunity to think freely about this. Change is an option for me because I have control of my own life. I don't have to change, but I can if I want to. I would love the same to be true for you.

Choosing to change

My journey of change started over thirty years ago, brought on by a traumatic childhood and abandonment by those I thought were going to rescue me. The trigger was something simple – a tune playing on the radio became my catalyst for change. Yes, the Billy Ocean song 'When the Going Gets Tough, the Tough Get Going' has a lot to answer for as it was this that inspired me to ask for help.

Where do I start? 'There but for the grace…' is a mantra I have carried with me all my life, even when I thought life couldn't get any harder than it was. I trusted and believed that whatever happened, I *was* lucky, despite enduring experiences that many people would find unbelievable. When you have nothing, anything is a bonus, even if it's merely the ability to detach and survive. Everything happens for a reason. I had to accept that there were others out there struggling through even worse circumstances than mine, and this acceptance brought power and meaning to my mantra. But while this mantra followed me at all times, there were occasions when I struggled to believe it.

I was born into a family with three older siblings, the last child my parents would have together. A few years after my birth, they separated and divorced, and while there was a stigma attached to being the child of a broken home in those days, I knew that this was ultimately going to be a positive thing to stop the cycles that had become established in my family home.

My childhood was made up of constant abuse of every kind you can imagine, from slavery to sexual assault. The tragic thing is that this was my norm during my formative years. It was only when I gave myself the opportunity to change my own life that I realised what had been happening to me was far from normal.

My early childhood consisted of daily violence. My father used his hands, fists and the end of a long leather greyhound lead with a wide collar to hit his child and wife. He, a 6-foot-tall adult man, thought nothing of beating a little girl. To a young child, every adult seems huge in every way, but to me, this man was particularly strong and overbearing. I lived with constant fear, never sleeping properly as a child, waiting for something bad to happen, to be disturbed in the night. When I heard footsteps striding across the landing, I used to pray that they would continue and not stop at my bedroom door. If they did, I hoped that the dog lying on my bed would protect me.

Subconsciously, I took this fear into my adult life, finally working to overcome it in my forties. I have always been a poor sleeper, and it was during a discussion one day with my husband about my insomnia that it all came together like a jigsaw puzzle, the last piece completing the picture.

While lack of sleep can be seen as a negative, it has enabled me to add a few extra hours to my day that have helped me turn my life around, allowing me to meditate and free my mind to other opportunities. I have also used the time to catch up with work and education into the early hours through reading, writing or listening to podcasts, audiobooks, talks – whatever stimulates my mind, even if I don't agree with it. I don't feel unhappy about being awake when everyone else is asleep; it's a quiet time that I make the most of, including taking time out for myself.

Taking control of your choices

The phrase 'life begins at forty' isn't true in my opinion. Life starts whenever you want it to.

Life is one big choice, but for a long time, I didn't realise that. Recognising this fact has taken my entire world in a new direction and allowed me to face whatever each day presents. While I may sometimes have to do things I don't want to do, nothing is as bad as the things I had to endure during my childhood. Everything I do now gives me an opportunity to choose to do my best and make the most of it. My diary rarely has a free slot, because I make sure to diarise the truly important things in life such as time with my family.

When I was a young child, my choices were made for me, as they are for most children. But the choices forced upon me were accompanied by fear; the trepidation of 'What if?'; the constant anxiety as I tried to avoid conflict, violence and abuse. This meant that the choices I made at the time were influenced by the negative dynamics of my environment, exaggerating the survival responses that most children have.

My choices since I've reached adulthood have been widespread, from picking the right man to share my life to admitting when I've made a poor decision. It may sound odd to write a list of requirements before entering into a relationship, but that's exactly what I did. After all, you wouldn't invest your money in a house if it was built on sand, so why invest your life in a relationship with equally unstable foundations? OK, it wasn't a huge list to start with, but I felt it was appropriate at the time, and I made the choice to write it on that basis. Over time, I have added to the list, including human values such as honesty, reliability, kindness, caring, faithfulness and loyalty, along with practical things like a good work ethic and financial stability. I needed to know that taking control of one's own destiny was a principle my life partner shared, and as a result of my list of requirements, I chose well and am currently celebrating thirty years of marriage.

My husband and I have grown together and developed our life skills way beyond anything either of us thought possible. Of course, we have had our ups and downs, just like any other couple, but we've always had a common goal to do our best and respect each other's choices, even if we don't agree with them. Whatever the circumstances, we've chosen to allow our diverse opinions to flourish to enhance our lives. I'm a lucky lady, but I have made my own luck, having put the legwork in.

In business, when employing someone new, I have given candidates an application form that allows them to share insights into their personality. The answers to questions such as 'What meal would you cook if your friends called round?' and 'Who has inspired you most in your life?' can say a lot about an individual. Looking at the choices they make in response to these questions is a great way to get a glimpse of a candidate's personality and values, which has allowed me to make good decisions about who joins my team and who doesn't.

Other choices which haven't always worked out so well concern who I wanted to partner with in business. Sometimes, my goal was so important to me, I forgot my basic principles such as respect at all times. Sadly, I had to learn to forgive these people for their lack of integrity and their abusive behaviour, but deep down, I really needed to forgive myself. I made a poor choice and paid for it both personally and financially, but what I gained were the invaluable learnings that can only come from the hard knocks in life. Fundamentally, this experience catapulted me towards a conviction that intuition is an important tool not to be ignored.

I made a choice, allowing selfish needs to get in the way, and I learned a life lesson. I was lucky to come out of it reasonably unscathed financially, suffering more from hurt pride than anything. The main takeaway, though, was that any choice, even a bad one, can lead to huge learnings.

I didn't listen to my instincts and took a stranger at their word, and I should have known better. Why would I enter into a working relationship with someone I don't know? This was a great reminder to stick to the basic principles I've developed – being true to the person I have become through many years of self-parenting, therapy, helping others and honesty – and use them to inform my choices.

TALES FROM THE MEMORY BANK

I recently had a conversation in my car on the way to the farm where I live. My travel companion asked a pertinent question with regards to honesty in relationships, wondering whether it could isolate me. In situations like choosing a business partner, I guess it might, but if I had stayed true to my values, then I would almost certainly have saved myself a lot of hurt, not to mention a few pounds in the bank.

This conversation made me realise that the choice to be truthful in all areas of my life has always served me well. It's only when I choose to dilute this principle that things go wrong. Then I need to take a step back, ask myself some testing questions and isolate my motives behind the choice and where they have come from.

If I make my choices based on honesty, then the reality is that I don't let myself down. What I have is an informed choice linked to my integrity and openness.

Home is where the heart is?

I've lived in a variety of different places, from County Durham to London and Manchester. I now choose to live in Somerset, but when I was a child, like many children, I didn't have any influence or choice in where I would live. Luckily for a lot of children, their parents put the kids' interests first. Unfortunately, the same wasn't true for me.

TALES FROM THE MEMORY BANK

As a kid, I moved from one type of accommodation to another, from local-authority homes to caravans to privately owned houses, depending on who my mother was living with at the time. I remember one evening in London not having a clue how to get to my latest home, having moved again after my mother had remarried. I had forgotten the address, there were no mobile phones back then and we didn't have a house phone at the time. I was wandering around south London, a scared and completely disorientated fourteen-year-old girl.

This kind of confusion was another 'norm' of my childhood. While some people would see a child having no stable home as a negative experience, I have turned it around. Now that I have the choice as to the home I live in, I love and appreciate it all the more. I understand the importance of having a secure home while appreciating it's OK not to have it, too. It's a valid choice.

My own children know that my home is their home. The last time we moved, we discussed it as a family, making sure the children were involved in the choice and checking they were happy with it. I wonder why many parents feel that it is their right to uproot a child from the security of the familiar without so much as a conversation with them about it.

I've had the luxury of helping and educating others to find a home, and I want to continue to do this. Knowing that someone has the choice to have a roof over their head, especially when the alternative is living on the streets, gives me a nice warm feeling.

Choices that affect others

I try to accept everyone as they are, neither judging their personality nor setting out to change them. If I am honest and open about my own feelings, I have the choice of whether to engage with the person or not.

I love the fact that I have learned to trust my intuition and know it won't let me down. I'm the one who lets my intuition down when I ignore its warnings and make poor choices. I was lured into thinking that my business partner was kind and trustworthy while the niggles in my tummy were telling me otherwise. I ignored the evidence and paid the price, making sure the experience became part of my learning.

My real sadness with regards to the times I have made a poor choice as a result of ignoring my intuition relates to the fact I often feel like I've let other people down. One bad apple can change good people into not so good, change people's opinions and actions, leading to a knock-on effect of destructive decision making based on insecurity. These are the risks I was taking whenever I ignored my gut feeling, and while they can lead to beneficial learning experiences, every time, I've felt like I have failed.

But failure is only a negative thing if you don't learn from the experience and ensure you don't repeat the same mistakes. My mistakes have made me stronger and equipped me with new skills. While it's not easy to rebuild after making a mistake, I have always chosen to do so. A builder does not give up on a house just because one wall isn't right; they simply tear down that wall and leave the others as they are. And that is exactly what I did. I chose to change the faulty wall while leaving everything else as it was.

I have seen people make poor choices, then do exactly the same thing again, hoping for a different outcome and being surprised when the negative result happens over and over. Learning from experience and not repeating destructive patterns is something that I learned about in my childhood as a result of being placed in incredibly vulnerable situations. This experience has served to remind me that all my choices have a bigger picture.

Being left to my own devices and having inconsistent parenting led to me feeling abandoned. With no positive role model, how could I become a good parent myself? With the help of a lot of support and therapy, I managed to repair the damage that my parents' life choices had caused to me. Thank goodness I recognised that I had the choice to take control of my own life.

It's a fact in life that we cannot change others, we can only change ourselves, but what we can do is advise others. There is a caveat, though. When I give instructions, guidance, advice – call it what you will – I always make sure to explain the reason behind it. I do this as a granny, mum, wife, mentor etc.

It is amazing how an explanation of your thinking and the reasons behind it can enhance your relationship with the people around you and turn instructions into choices. Personally, whenever I have been told to do something without hearing the reasoning behind the instruction, it has generally resulted in me either not listening or rebelling. There's never a positive outcome; even if I obey the command, it tends to be resentfully.

What, then, should you base your reasoning on when you want others to do something? That's simple: always remain true to your values. The difficulty is knowing what to base your values on. Only you can answer that, but I can offer some guidance.

If a person chooses money and status as the bedrock of their values, never reflecting on what or who is truly important, the strategic decisions they make throughout their life often lead to them, and the people around them, always being on the edge. No one then benefits from the warm, fluffy feeling we only get when we have chosen to be true to ourselves and our own grace. If we're not true to our inner values, how can we possibly respect anyone else's? How can we build fulfilling relationships on firm foundations?

The inner voice

My internal conversations often highlight both my imagined and true self, allowing my journey through life to be an internal battle and a welcome break from my surroundings. In this respect, the inner voice can be perceived as a level of mental ill health as well as good health. This dichotomy may seem crazy, and I have spent many hours talking to people who think they are going mad because of the voices in their heads when, in fact, we all have these voices. The choice is whether we listen to what they say and act upon it or completely ignore it.

The mind is a wonderful tool. It can project the future and manufacture hopes, dreams and horrors. It can help to ensure the choices we make are informed, but only if we take notice of the evidence it lays before us. What is in front of us and what has happened in the past gives us invaluable clues as to what could happen; we just have to decide which path to take.

People who have been told their inner voices are linked to an acute mental disorder can be tortured by this conversation. I wonder how many of these tortured people could have a nicer life if only those purporting to help them reached out with support and love rather than negativity. I've had the privilege of doing just this and have seen people, when given the option to change their relationship with their inner self, enjoy the freedom of acceptance without retribution.

TALES FROM THE MEMORY BANK

I remember working with a client who'd grown up with little acceptance from either parent. Her internal conversation was centred around insecurity and not knowing what real parenting was, and as a result, she became a hyper-alert but critical parent herself. She regarded everything as danger.

This young woman had little respect for her own value and would regularly self-harm. My time with her was purely spent working on her acceptance of who she was and her inner voices. Now, she has a strong positive influence in her community and no longer self-harms.

Drugs and alcohol – they're choices too

If we decide to dull the brain and our inner voice with drugs or alcohol, this can only make our journey to self-acceptance harder. The influence mind-altering substances have on our inner conversations and our responses to them brings controversy and confusion, and makes a complete mess of the roadmap in our head. It would be like a barrister representing us in court after having had a few shots of whisky or pints of lager or glasses of wine. Any clarity of expression would be compromised, and our case would likely be lost as soon as our barrister opened their mouth. Our inner voice is our life barrister. I urge you to respect and listen to yours, rather than hiding it behind mind-altering substances.

Yes, I made poor choices as a young woman, using mood-altering chemicals including alcohol to inhibit the internal chatter that forced itself in through my own life experiences. As I didn't have the maturity to challenge or delete the negative conversation, I took the easy option to silence the inner voices. In reality, though, I was replacing one conversation with an even more negative script. Now I was making decisions based on a dishonest internal conversation, influenced by my own bad experiences, poor decision making and lack of insight on how to change, and the outcome was never good. By the time I was twenty-one, I had not only got married, but was separated. With two kids to look after, I was a homeless addict. Good choices? I think not!

Of course, your mind can play tricks on you, but the reality is it's your mind, no one else's. You and you alone start the inner conversation and choose whether or not to act on it. This is where intuition can step in, if you let it.

If a confusion of thoughts is bouncing around my head, my intuition is my backup team. It's the fixer, the mechanic in my choice bank, waiting for me to drive away fully informed of what is right or wrong. It's just down to me to listen to the advice it gives and make sure I top up the oil and water accordingly. The trouble is, who listens to the mechanics all the time? That's why we can all make poor choices. The important thing is to make sure the inner voice, the mechanic, isn't silenced behind the chatter brought about by drugs and alcohol, which never helped anyone to make wise and informed choices.

Choosing when to let go

I'm in the change game, constantly looking at the potential to help people make different choices and develop new coping strategies. This improves not only their lives but also those of the people around them. For this reason, I make a lot of choices based on the potential I see in others rather than the finished product.

Change is ongoing, but only if the individual wants it to be that way. While I recognise my standards are high, this isn't a bad thing. It keeps me on my toes and gives others hope.

I meet a lot of people who believe that their past defines their future. While I identify with this and realise it may be the case, it can be shaped in a different way. My personal journey started with my dysfunctional childhood, but I took positive influences from the people who didn't abuse me and did my best to leave the traits of the others behind.

My mother wasn't the best, but she taught me well in some areas. Her negative choices reinforced in me the importance of always being there for my own children, whatever the circumstances. It would have been easier for me to walk away when I was at my worst, but I remember the feelings of abandonment I had as a little girl, the deep pain of loss that I haven't experienced since, and I never wanted that for my children.

TALES FROM THE MEMORY BANK

There was a time in my early life when I didn't know whether my mother was dead or alive. I prayed every day and night, hoping she would come back to me, send a card – anything to show she cared. Nothing came for many years, and when it did, it was temporary.

While I do think about her sometimes and wish my relationship with her could have been different, the reality is I cannot change her. None of us can change another person; we can only change ourselves. My mother was not willing to change for me, so it was my choice whether to continue to resent this or accept and let it go. The latter was the option I chose because I no longer wanted to suffer the rejection and the internal conversation about what I'd done wrong to deserve to be treated in this way. As an adult, I realised I hadn't done anything wrong; it was all down to her poor choices. My inner child had to choose to let the emotional trauma go and walk away.

At times, I have held on to resentments from my past, but I know this never serves my ongoing choices well. The abuse and terror I experienced as a child at the hands of my father have sometimes made me fearful of men, but they have also equipped me to be resilient. I know nothing anyone else may do would be worse than what he did. This has taught me to make sure I never behave like him, and that shame doesn't have to control me. I don't have to be violent to get my point across and it's OK to make mistakes.

This choice to repair myself is important as sadly, my father never admitted his faults, so he never earned the opportunity to be part of my beautiful life. If he had, would I, or indeed could I have forgiven him for what he did? I truly don't know if I could. Would I have been able to trust he wouldn't do the same to my children?

The choices I made ensured there would be no ongoing repetition in my life of the family pattern of abusing others and blaming them for it. While I may have had a part to play in different scenarios from my past, the reality and truth prevails in my heart. Adult clarity has brought with it the realisation that sometimes, others will perpetuate bad behaviour from their childhood, and then try to deflect the blame for their choices on to others. For me, the opportunity to be open about what happened was painful, but it made me aware of the choice of truth.

You don't have to be your parents or your parents' parents. You just have to choose the path you feel is right for you and change it if necessary.

TALES FROM THE MEMORY BANK

My nan and grandad are a strong influence from my past. When I was little, I lived with them for a few short stable times in the chaos of my childhood. They were amazing people who loved me unconditionally. I was allowed to be a child, have friends and fun, eat nice things. Ham, egg and chips was the first meal I remember us eating together. I had never had anything so amazingly yummy before.

One day, Grandad picked me up from school – not something I recollect my parents ever doing. It was a cracking sunny day, and on the way home, we took a detour to a local chocolate shop called. It had a beautiful dark olde worlde frontage with gold lettering and large windows with bullseye glass.

Walking into the shop, I was so excited. Grandad bought me an ice cream, the first one I had ever had, then held my hand all the way back to the flat. To this day, my heart fills with joy and gratitude for this moment in time. My grandparents didn't have a lot, but they were willing to share it with me with no expectation of being paid back in any way. It was the pure, unconditional love that I wish could be the reality for every child.

Now I'm a granny myself, I love picking up my grandchildren from school, and then a visit to the local shop for treats. It feels like such a position of trust. I just hope my own grandchildren will carry a fondness for this special memory into their adult life.

The influence of choices

The influence of my choices is clear to me. Remaining clean and sober – by which I mean sane thinking and acting to prevent abuse, unkindness or harm to others – is at the top of my list. I have seen many a family traumatised because of the poor choices that others have made, either with or without thought for the consequences today and in the long term, then repeated time and time again.

Sometimes, it's the failure to make a choice that impacts on others. Continuing along a path of negativity without insight from an outsider's perspective can leave a trail of devastation which sometimes lasts a lifetime and on through the generations to come, which is why I have chosen to offer that outsider's perspective time and time again.

Did I want the influence of the choices my parents made to continue into my children's lives? No, I did not! While I have taken on a huge responsibility, I have developed my choices through my need not to repeat the same patterns of my past, instigating change to give my children the chance to break away from these patterns. My children have all chosen to have children of their own and, unlike me, they had the grounding to be able to choose when to have their children. They all have careers, a level of financial security and a permanent roof over their heads, unlike my experience of homelessness. My choice to break away from the destructive behaviours of my parents has gone a long way towards enabling my children to have the foundations to make measured and informed choices for themselves.

The entrenchment that some people choose to stay in is so sad to see. Thank goodness I have been able to build my resource bank up so I can cope with anything that comes my way. My choice was to work on my resilience, even though this was born out of the pure survival instinct of my childhood. I have had to cull some of my choices and re-evaluate their influence on my life and the lives of those I love along the way, and this is a process I regularly check. I work hard on not being complacent. 'That will do' doesn't often feature in my world unless I've explored all the options and decided I have done all I can.

Lowering your standards to meet those of others is a cop out. I don't ever let the standards and choices of other people influence me; what I do is choose to move on in my own way towards a positive impact.

Fundamentally, if your intentions are good, then your choices will be too. Liking the 'I' rather than the 'we' brings an inner peace and a selection of choices, rather than handing responsibility, and the blame, over to another person.

Why don't some people change their negative ways? While I find this immensely frustrating, especially when I can predict the consequences of their reluctance to develop their inner self and make better choices, I see it as their choice not to. But where does this choice come from? Is it fear or lack of motivation? Or is it because someone else is trying to influence them by taking their right to choose away from them?

TALES FROM THE MEMORY BANK

I was working with a young woman who was in a fairly new relationship. Unfortunately, her partner was increasingly putting demands on her to make different choices. When we explored the reason behind this, asking why her partner expected her to make a choice that wasn't in her best interests, we realised it was her partner who actually wanted to make changes.

A choice has to be just that. It has to be personal and true to each individual's inner values. If it isn't, it won't be what the person really wants and is unlikely be sustainable. And as I said to the young woman I was working with, if you want to be in a relationship with a certain person, why would you want to take their choices away? It would only lead to them living a lie, which in turn leads to resentment and long-term pain.

My work has exposed me to many similar cases and the sad reality it brings with it. Taking choices away from someone steals their peace of mind, and can influence those around them, too, sometimes destroying the bedrock of a family, home or work environment, bringing with it even more trauma.

TALES FROM THE MEMORY BANK

A particular case comes to mind where I received a call from a devastated parent who had found their son had taken his own life. The emotional trauma in this parent's voice still haunts me.

The son had spoken to me two days before his death, asking if he could come back to see me; but in the end he obviously chose not to. How different the picture could have been if he had felt able to seek help and receive it; his parent, and his wife and children, would have had a future with the man they loved.

Sadly, this isn't the only case I have experienced of a person with much to give taking their own life rather than seek help.

The sadness every suicide leaves behind cannot be measured or repaired. To find that a loved one has taken their own life leaves scars that rarely heal. While I understand that some people may feel they have no other option, I wish they were able to play the tape forward and realise the effect their actions will have on people they love, and seek help rather than take this final step.

Telling lies, being unfaithful, stealing peace of mind from others – in my experience, this can only leave a trail of destruction. A good decision based on helping those around you outweighs self-preservation. I have made decisions to benefit others at my own expense because I know I can heal myself. Knowing and understanding that I have made a choice that's well thought through and true to myself has allowed me the privilege and long-term rewards of seeing people grow.

Any regrets?

Would I change anything about my life? Simple answer: yes.

I wish I'd had the perfect parents. Maybe that would have saved me from a lot of heartache, but I've used my traumatic childhood to my advantage and taken the lessons I've learned from it to help me grow. Have I made lots of mistakes along the way? Of course, I have; I'm human. I got pregnant as a kid, but do I regret having my beautiful son followed by my amazing daughter? Not for a second. If I'd been a little older when they were born, I may have been better prepared as a parent, but I have always been filled with the love for my kids that I was denied in my own childhood.

Do I regret getting married at seventeen? No, I learned a lot. Even though I was divorced by my early twenties, it gave me an insight into what marriage is about so I could make a better job of it in future. I've worked incredibly hard on my current marriage rather than walking away. Hopefully, this has helped my kids approach marriage with the same values.

Was using mood-altering drugs a poor choice? Of course it was, but it led me to seek out a group of people from all over the world who understand why I made that choice. They don't judge me; they have simply helped me to put some things into perspective and change the course of the choices I was making. This help is always at hand whenever I want it, making me realise I am not alone with my sadness and loss anymore.

Do I regret going to rehab? Yes and no. The staff were sometimes punitive and unkind, shaming me so much that I struggled to forgive myself. But I chose to go to sustain my recovery, and the bad experience I had there helped me realise I never want to go back. It also gave me a dream: one day, I would open a rehab facility where people are truly cared for; a recovery home with a recovery family. This I have accomplished with the support of my loved ones.

Wow, how lucky I am to be able to help people make changes in their choices for the future, choices which impact on them, their families and their families' families. Of the hundreds of people who have entered the facility, if I'd only helped ten to achieve what they wanted, then that would have been amazing. But between you and me, I'm delighted to say the success rates are way higher than that.

Do I regret remarrying and having another child? Far from it – this was the icing on the cake for me. It gave me an opportunity to show that I had made the choice to be a good wife and mother, providing guidance and freedom for my amazing family. Although I was dreading going through giving birth and all the sleepless nights again, hoping I wouldn't be a failure, I haven't been. I have chosen not to be.

I have made mistakes on the journey. My choices haven't always the best. But I have raised three wonderful kids and watched them grow into adults who have made the choice to contribute to their local community and be caring, kind and fantastic individuals.

Do I regret not keeping in touch with people from my past who never took responsibility for their actions? No, I don't. I made some poor choices, but I have made amends by breaking the mould. My kids have not repeated the patterns because they have always been loved, not abused in any way. And I respect my husband and our marriage vows.

I recently learned, three months after the event, that my father had died, and the newspapers were not kind about him – confirmation of the pain he caused not only to his children, but also to others in the community. I wish I had been brave enough to let society know the kind of person he was, possibly saving others from suffering at his hands, but I was always worried I wouldn't be believed. It's a choice I regret, and when I finally opened up to my children about my past, it was one of the most painful experiences of my life. Perhaps if I had been open from the start, I wouldn't have had to go through this uncomfortable part of my journey.

Today, I choose to continue to grow from my and others' experiences and knowledge, remembering to consult my inner voice so I can be sure I'm following my own path. What I do will always impact on those around me, so I can choose to make my choices either informed or not. I can consider others or not. I can play the whole tape or not. There will be a consequence to whatever I choose, so I just have to remember that it's not all about me.

TWO
Courage

Courage is a word reminiscent of lions and tigers, or those who have fought in wars and been given the label of a hero. I have images of a knight in shining armour rescuing a princess from a tower, slaying the fearsome dragon so everyone can live happily ever after. But in my reality, courage is something different.

The courage I have experienced envelops me with pride and hope. It manifests itself in many ways, often unrecognised by society, and has touched me and those around me.

The courage to be a child

I remember spending most of my childhood in fear. Fear of the known – fear of recurring abuse and lack of love. For me, courage meant the everyday resilience to survive the horrendous experience I was going through: a ceaseless battle against what would have been headline news nowadays. Unbelievable acts of cruelty became the norm, and it takes a tremendous amount of courage to survive a norm like that.

A daily trudge through household chores prevented me from having much interaction with other children. I was never allowed to play with other children, which is such an important part of learning life skills; my only opportunity to meet people my own age was at school, so while many children might have moaned and groaned about attending lessons every day, I thanked goodness for it. Sleepovers, tea and parties with friends were unheard of for me. I didn't go to one single birthday party throughout my entire childhood, and I certainly never had one of my own.

TALES FROM THE MEMORY BANK

The inner resources of children are quite amazing. From somewhere, I found the courage to sneak out to play during the school holidays, praying I wouldn't be caught and covering every track just in case. I remember going grass sledging on a cardboard box, which was fantastic fun; I laughed like I'd never laughed before. The only problem was when things went wrong – I cut myself on barbed wire and had to make up some lie, saying one of the dogs (my father kept greyhounds to feed his gambling addiction) pulled me over. I hated the deceit, but was so grateful to be a child, even if it was for a short time.

Another disaster happened when I sneaked a friend in to play at our house while my father and stepmother were out. Unfortunately, when he left, he shut the back door rather too forcefully and the window smashed. I remember lying in bed, waiting for my father to return, knowing the window had been smashed and fearing the consequences. Day-to-day abuse was normal, so he was always looking for an excuse to up the violence.

When he came to my bedroom, I found the courage to tell him the broken window was my fault and had been an accident. I said I was scared he wouldn't love me anymore if I'd not waited up to tell him. For the first time in my life, my father surprised me. He actually let it go, although I'm not sure if this didn't subsequently make things worse. After that, I knew he had the capacity to be fair-minded and trust me; he just chose never to tap into this capacity again.

In Chapter 1, I touched on the fact that throughout my life, I have made choices for the benefit of others, even if they were detrimental to me, as I knew I was strong enough to recover from the consequences. I made such choices a lot during my formative years, regularly covering for my siblings by doing extra chores to mitigate the risk of the constant violence as our father looked for any excuse to reinforce his power over the household. I was the one to step forward, finding the courage even then to be true to who I am, which helped me survive. I was always full of energy, so extra work never got in the way. It would be a lie to say I never felt any resentment, but it soon passed.

TALES FROM THE MEMORY BANK

After my mother left us, I was constantly hungry, so much so that in the end, I didn't know what was hunger and what was normal. I would steal milk from our neighbours' doorsteps – sorry, it was me, but it was because I was hungry – and occasionally food from the local shop for the same reason. While I knew it was wrong, I was a ravenously hungry little girl who knew no one else was going to provide for her.

Yes, I was frightened that I would be caught stealing, but then my courage and my desperation kicked in and I did it all the same. It might seem like a negative courage, but survival is the most basic of human needs. Goodness knows what I would have done if I had been caught; on reflection, I reckon local people knew what I was doing, and why, and they turned a blind eye. I thank them if they did.

The courage to thrive

Showing that children can find the courage not just to survive but to thrive in the most appalling of circumstances, I shone at school. I allowed myself to bask in the praise and recognition my teachers gave me for being a hard worker, even though this was never recognised at home.

TALE FROM THE MEMORY BANK

At school, I enjoyed playing the violin, becoming accomplished enough to lead the orchestra. Unfortunately, but inevitably, I had to give it up as it interfered with my responsibilities at home; I had reached the point where my violin lessons and the concerts the orchestra played took place outside of school hours, and this was not allowed. I can't deny I was disappointed, but I had to take it without a tantrum; I would never show my feelings in front of my father. It took courage to cope with the disappointment and sense of loss I felt.

I recently picked up a violin that belonged to a client. While I was rubbish, I could still remember how to hold it properly and play a little. Perhaps one day, I will find the courage to try again. I'm smiling as I write this.

My mother didn't give me much, but one gift I did receive from her was the ability to sing. It wasn't until I went into therapy that I linked the songs I've always had in my head, 'Summertime' by Ella Fitzgerald being a favourite, with the fact that my mother used to sing them so beautifully. I was part of the choir at school and was regularly asked to sing solo parts, but I could never say yes, as yet again, I wasn't allowed to take part in concerts. Even when I was offered a scholarship at a music school, I had to turn it down. Once more, my courage got me through my disappointment, which was by now as big as the largest lake in the world. But I didn't allow myself to be broken by it.

Many years later, my husband encouraged me to take the risk and try singing again. The pride I felt when I passed my Grade 8 singing exam was fantastic.

The courage to survive

The cowardly lion in *The Wizard of Oz* comes to mind whenever I think of courage. The lion wants nothing more than to be brave, but it turns out that he had courage deep inside himself all the time; he just needed to go on a journey to find it.

Like the cowardly lion, a little freckled ginger-haired girl had to follow her own Yellow Brick Road and find her courage. As that little girl, I never had particularly nice clothes – just hand-me-downs that really should have been put in the bin. My socks were never white, my pants were always shabby, my body was black and blue from the many beatings I endured, so changing for PE in school was a nightmare. I wanted to hide in the corner, but I didn't; I braved it and faced up to my fears. If I was in the corner, I would be hiding my abilities as well as my shame.

TALES FROM THE MEMORY BANK

One day, I was pulled over by one of my father's dogs that I was out walking. It was late in the evening and my father was gambling like he did every night; the dog, who weighed more than I did, became overexcited, dragging me to the ground. I hurt my side. The pain was excruciating.

When I went inside to the bathroom at the dog track to clean myself up, I saw the extent of the damage. My side had been cut open near my hip and I could see the bone, but when I showed my father, all he did was get a plaster from somewhere, and that was it. Forty-five years later, I still bear a 2-inch scar.

The next day at school, I asked if I could be excused from PE. When the teacher asked why, I showed them what had happened, but just like my father and his sticking plaster, all they did was cover it up. I do wonder how different my life would have been if someone had shown the courage to report the obvious neglect and mistreatment that was happening to me. I hope that today, things may be different, but in my job, I can't help but know that some so-called professionals will still do anything to avoid having to confront an awkward and difficult situation.

Sharing this tale from my memory bank has been an emotional experience. Who knows what pain I could have been spared had one person in authority, just one, had the courage to take my side?

My obvious neglect went either unnoticed or ignored. While this enabled the family tradition of saying nothing about what was going on at home, it also reinforced my belief that the abuse I was suffering was normal.

The courage to endure

My whole childhood was mapped out for me: get up as early as possible so my father's sleep wasn't disturbed by a hungry dog; muck out the dog kennels; feed and walk the greyhounds. Make tea for him. Clean and tidy the house before going to school. If my father had remembered to get any bread, I might be able to sneak a bite to eat; otherwise, I left the house hungry.

In the afternoon, I had to come home straight away – no after-school activities for me – and repeat the dog routine with a longer walk. If there was food in the house, I'd be able to make (myself) some dinner, then I'd fetch whichever dog my father was racing that night and sit in a darkened car park all evening to make sure the dog didn't chew the car. We'd get home between 10.30–11.30pm, my father's mood depending on whether the dog had won or lost, then I'd have to sort the dogs out before going to bed.

But that wasn't the worst of it. From time to time, my father would perform acts on me that I have no desire to describe. The first time it occurred, he said it was his way of managing the trauma of my mother leaving us. I was little and believed him; it was only later that the residual nasty smell and pain convinced me that something very wrong had happened to me.

My father was violent to the degree of grievous bodily harm. He had no regard for anyone but himself. Sadly, the courts thought it was perfectly OK for this type of man to have custody of his children. My mother came and went in my life. After my father remarried, I acquired a stepmother with whom I had a very difficult relationship.

I still ask myself why a person would treat anyone so badly, let alone a little girl. But my courage to endure shone through.

Many years ago, I read a book called *The Courage to Heal*.[1] This book enlightened me, giving me a different perspective on how I had developed survival mechanisms to endure whatever life sent me. My faith and hope that it would change one day gave me the resilience to withstand shaming and abuse at its worst Even though some would see the way I adapted to my surroundings as people pleasing, I saw it as a survival

---

1   E Bass, L Davis *The Courage to Heal: A guide for women survivors of childhood sexual abuse* (Vermilion, 2002)

skill. Without this skill, I'm not sure where my path would have taken me.

The courage to escape

The trouble was, my norm wasn't getting any better. I didn't want to leave as this was all I had ever known, while the idea of running away was scary and unknown – but if I had stayed, I probably wouldn't be writing these words now. When I left with my sister, I was terrified and it took all my courage to agree to get on a train to London, not knowing what was going to happen. To this day, all I remember are feelings of sadness and fear, and then my courage stepped in and prevented me from turning around and going back to a home full of pain.

I am glad I took the step of running away from home with my sister and seeking refuge with our mother. She had a beautiful home and worked really hard to fill it with nice things, but the reality was she had never been there for us. She had no idea about the bullying I'd endured at school, or the fact I had adopted negative coping strategies and attention-seeking behaviour, or that I suffered constant internal torture. It took all my courage to get through each day.

As I write this, I am picturing my thirteen-year-old self, catapulted into a completely new life with a group of strangers. The different men who regularly came and went meant there was no feeling of stability in the home, and battles at school resulted in constant truancy. I thought I had got away from violence, but it seemed I had jumped from the frying pan and into the fire. It took a lot of courage for me to call the police to deal with the alcoholic man my mother had brought home who was tearing the place apart.

The courage to grow

During my two years in London, I met some amazing people, one being a local café owner who, along with his family, gave me a place of sanctuary that I had never experienced before. For once, I had a positive male role model, one who would never dream of forcing himself on me. Instead, he gave me work and always paid a fair wage, which allowed me a level of freedom to buy clothes and music. Sadly, it also gave me the means to buy mood-altering drugs.

Thanks to this good man, I was able to establish a strong work ethic, which has served me well throughout my life. If I could find him today, I would say thank you. Thank you for taking a chance on a girl who obviously needed help and support. He gave me the space to grow into a young woman, teaching me the values of business ethics, honesty and always treating people with respect, whatever the circumstances.

Having been given the freedom back then to try my best and develop my skills, I can still rustle up a good meal out of next to nothing, being careful about the produce and not wasting anything. I recently catered a light breakfast for sixty people and a close friend observed how easy I made it look. I suppose for me it is, but this is down to the teachings of a man who gave me courage to believe in myself and grow.

TALES FROM THE MEMORY BANK

The café I worked in during my time in London was opposite a theatre, so I met a whole host of interesting people from all walks of life. Actors and actresses, educators and hard workers graced the safe environment the café held for me. They encouraged me to socialise with them and I was always welcomed.

When I was asked to work for a local greengrocer who had a delivery round, I started going to Covent Garden in the early hours, then helping with the deliveries. I loved it and it provided me with even more much-needed money to pay for food, clothes etc. Sadly, though, this opportunity came to an abrupt end after a bad encounter with another greengrocer working around the corner from where I lived.

This greengrocer's shop was beautiful, always laid out immaculately. The fruit was layered on a variety of coloured tissue paper expertly folded to enhance its beauty. The flowers stood tall and grand, showing their colours like parading soldiers. I loved the aesthetics of the whole thing, and to this day, I still like a good fruit-and-veg shop.

The downside was the man who owned the shop. While appearing to be respectable and friendly, I think he was a paedophile. A cunning man, he became involved with my mother so she was blinded by his charm, offering to help her in her times of need, driving a truck for us when we needed to move. But all the time, he was grooming me, a vulnerable child who no one kept an eye on, so I could disappear for some time and it would not be noticed.

After charming me, giving me work to help with my living expenses, making himself aware of my circumstances, he set up an arrangement to meet me at a certain location. When I arrived, he was a little bit jittery, which I found odd. I hadn't seen this side of him before; I just thought he was a kind man like the café owner who'd taken me under his wing.

He told me he was intending on meeting me at his flat. He was a married man with a house and family, so why would he have a flat? And why would I need to meet him there? I was always compliant and doing as I was told, but that night, I felt frightened for some reason. Intuition, perhaps, was telling me that something wasn't right. Whatever it was, I didn't go and never saw him again. To my knowledge, neither did my mother.

The next day, I told the greengrocer whose delivery round I was doing what I thought was happening.

He never came to pick me up again to do the round. In fact, both men disappeared. So putting two and two together, I figured I had come up with the right answer. It was the first time I had either stood my ground or told someone about what I thought was going on. I had grown in courage, realising I could make my own choices and was not a commodity for people to use and abuse as they pleased.

Saying no to people has always been a challenge for me, but this was one of the times my courage shone through. Thank goodness for intuition, although the experience of having lived with an abuser for most of my life had equipped me to recognise one. Even my father gave me some tools to help me grow.

The courage to welcome new life

My life in London was coming to an end, or so I thought. I was moving to Somerset with my mother and her third husband to start a new life, but I was dreading this. Having not really had much contact with my mother throughout my life, I couldn't get my head around the idea of playing happy families.

I was under strict instructions not to disclose any of my past, and so I lived a life of pretence – I had to tell people that my mother's husband was my father. Thanks to my negative experiences with men, I was not in the habit of trusting in a father figure. As far as my mother was concerned, whatever may or may not happen in the future, she had made many promises in the past and never come up with the goods.

Our 'new life' didn't start well. Once again, I had to learn to live with complete strangers. I went to a school where most kids hadn't even travelled on a train, let alone from the other side of the country, so I was a bit of a novelty. The inevitable resultant bullying brought one horrendous experience after another; I wasn't liked by the girls in the school, and while I had learned not to be the kind of person to judge, I didn't see a lot to like in them, either. I tried my best, but I was so unhappy, like a fish out of water. I was unable to form normal relationships, and yet again, believing I had any worth became a struggle.

Then my new start in Somerset came to an abrupt end when I became pregnant with my first child and escaped back to London. There was enormous pressure on me to have a termination, but this wasn't something I wanted to happen. I was nearly seventeen and didn't have much of a start in life to offer a newborn, but one of the most courageous steps I took in life was the decision to not have an abortion or give my beautiful son up for adoption. As my baby's father came from a strong Roman Catholic background, the shame brought on by the pregnancy was tough to endure, but together we worked it out and decided to marry. Even though our marriage didn't work out, I'm so glad I stuck to my guns.

When it was obvious my marriage was not in a happy place, I left London with my two children and went back to live with my mother, carrying on where I'd left off and following wherever my mother and stepfather led. Did I do this to people please or take a courageous step into a new life? At the time, I was lonely and scared, and an old pattern soon re-established itself. My negative coping strategies came back into play and I people pleased all day long, trying to keep the peace. I was saddened, ashamed and mortified that my marriage hadn't worked out, but I knew I had to find the courage to carry on and build a good life for my children.

The courage to change

While I appreciate the home my mother and stepfather gave me and my children, it wasn't an easy time. I wasn't the best mother; I became addicted to drugs and got many things wrong, but when I realised that I needed to change my ways, I found the courage to go to rehab. This gave me the insights I needed into how not to be and permission to recognise the true reality of my life.

TALES FROM THE MEMORY BANK

The first time I ever told anyone a little of what had happened in my childhood, their response wasn't great. But while some of the other residents in rehab thought that I was lying, I knew by then that what had happened to me as a child wasn't OK, and this knowledge subsequently gave me the courage to talk about it in therapy after treatment.

The experience of rehab gave me the courage to make changes which have been ongoing throughout my life. I've gained the courage to be who I am, becoming more aware of myself, my choices, hopes and dreams. I have since carried on working on myself, being caring but honest, allowing my true personality to appear.

I made a decision at that point in my life not to hold on to other people's dishonesties. There were some scary people in rehab who had always been unscrupulous and continued to be so when in treatment. It took all my courage to report what I believed was going on, and I wasn't well liked among my peers for it. But this courage to face up to and deal with the reality that everything isn't always as it should be gave me a solid foundation for my life.

My experience in a rehab environment that was punitive, aggressive and unkind gave me a dream, too: a dream that one day, I would open my own rehab facility to provide support, hope and care for people at their most vulnerable. I had the privilege of fulfilling this dream in 2006 – wow, what an amazing experience.

It's a wonderful feeling to know that you've had the courage to take a risk and do something that may fail, but may also make your dreams come true.

The courage to move on

Having had terrible experiences as a child and a not so good first marriage, I had no idea about relationships, so I needed the courage to find out exactly what it was I really wanted from a man. Therapy came in handy here, as that was when I started my list of requirements. I'd never have thought to do that on my own.

I wrote a list of what I wanted and didn't want in a relationship, and when I met someone who had the potential to be a significant other, I expected him to meet the majority of the positives. Having ascertained my values, I wove them into my requirements, which led me to marrying a person with the same values. Some might say my list was too demanding, others might find it funny, but it did the trick.

My values-based requirements consist of honesty, openness, caring, support and financial security. Yes, I want to share my life with someone who regards money in the same way I do. From the moment I made my list, I believed I had the right to ask for all these requirements to be met as well as the courage to follow it through.

TALES FROM THE MEMORY BANK

Having been out of education since the age of thirteen, I found the courage to return. I was terrified; I didn't feel able to write an essay, never mind put it all on a computer, but I forced myself through the barrier of fear and submitted my work.

I was supported by my family and course tutors, even though I know I wasn't an easy student, and I went on to graduate as a fully fledged counsellor, bringing together my intuitive skills, compassion and care. Today, when new clients come into rehab saying they can't read, write or communicate their feelings, I know from my own experience that they can be helped and supported to achieve this, even if it feels miles away at the moment.

Thank goodness for courage and self-belief. Taking the first step is the start of an amazing journey.

Having another child was something I was unsure about. I hadn't had the best experiences of pregnancy, vomiting from conception to birth, so did I really want to go through that again?

It was a courageous step to decide to expand my family with my husband, but it's paid me back over and over again, even though I did vomit all the way through. My poor family had a lot to tolerate as this wasn't an easy ride for any of us. Giving birth was pretty horrendous, too, with the umbilical cord wrapped around our little chap's neck, but we all survived.

Having had the courage to move my life on from the dark times, I am able to say I'm successful in my accomplishments as a businesswoman, a wife, a mother and a friend. I have the courage to say what needs to be said when others step back, act when others won't and take risks even if they don't always work out. I have the courage to stick to my principles, and make educated decisions to change them if need be. I have the courage to say if I don't know the answer to something and investigate when I can.

When times have been bad, switching off would have been a lovely option, but I have always had the courage not to do this. Rather, I carry on in spite of the difficulties. I have the courage to break away from the dysfunctional family of my childhood and not repeat the mistakes they made. This has been hard, but it's brought the rewards of honesty and wholesome relationships. I have the courage to choose whether to forgive or not to forgive, to decide for myself and believe in my own values instead of bending them to fit in. I am who I am, and truthfully, I believe I'm a good person with little malice inside.

Courage has been a constant throughout my life. I no longer live a lie and allow people to abuse me, or others. I am the person who won't settle for second best. I'm happy to be poor or wealthy, as long as I have the courage to share what I have with those around me and continue to be true to myself.

THREE
Gratitude

G ratitude can change the world. When we don't have it, our environment can feel like an angry place, often putting us in a position of victim.

Where do I start to explain my journey with gratitude? As I lie in my bed in a beautiful part of the country, snuggled under a cosy duvet, my amazing husband by my side, I consider that life couldn't be any better. Or could it?

First memories of gratitude

What exactly is the value in having gratitude? I've always felt how lucky I am. Even if it was just the night as a child when I wasn't disturbed in my bedroom or beaten with the dog lead by my father, I could always find things to be grateful for.

Those who compare and moan don't recognise the power of gratitude. Those who resent someone else's successes rarely identify their own. These people need to learn to be grateful for all the good things in their lives. Only then can they be true to themselves and achieve their full potential.

My life as a child was like being in a washing machine that kept getting its cycle interrupted. I was either waiting for the water to enter the machine or bracing myself for the spin cycle, bringing horrendous chaos into my world. That's how unbalanced my life was. The dysfunctional actions of the people who were meant to care for me created this environment, and as a little girl, I had no choice but to suck it up. And that's what I did. When life was this bad, believe me, being grateful for the little things was never a problem.

TALES FROM THE MEMORY BANK

A hot meal, or indeed food at all – something many take for granted – was an amazing treat after my mother left. She was an awesome cook, so I really missed her cooking. To this day, her meat and potato pie with beetroot is the epitome of yum for me.

My eldest sister had a birthday party when our mother was still around, and the food she had was amazing. Everything was in batter, or so I remember, from onion rings to bananas, and it's the type of food I still crave. I never had a party until I was old enough to host my own, but I didn't feel hard done by. I was just grateful for the memories that we were able to share.

I recently had a conversation with someone who said they don't ever feel grateful for their own achievements, let alone those of others. That is so sad. This person never feels the pride and joy of sharing special moments because they see no value in it and can't remember ever doing so. It's not surprising, then, that they don't connect with themselves or others. If you do not have a relationship with things, events, people, the world must be really lonely.

Gratitude for education

I loved school until I moved to London, when the actions of bullies denied me the privilege of an education. Today, I feel such gratitude that my children and grandchildren, and all children in the UK, have the right to education.

When I was a child, my father would keep us away from school if he had hit us in the wrong place and the bruising showed, or when he was hiding from someone he owed money to. Not going to school was a huge wrench for me – school was my escape from the reality of life, somewhere I could make my mark through being an achiever and enjoying positive recognition, and I was so grateful for this. Perhaps one of the reasons things went so terribly wrong for me was that school was no longer a safe place to be when I went to London.

Before the bullies ruined it all, school brought play, friends, sport, education, books and a sense of belonging and being cared for. OK, the teachers all ignored the obvious signs of my neglect, but that didn't take away from the fact I loved school in my early years. To this day, I'm thankful that I had the choice to go.

TALES FROM THE MEMORY BANK

Recently, I took a trip to Vietnam. I'm not the one who instigates our holiday schedules; to me, home is always more attractive than getting on a plane and travelling around the world, but I recognise that travel educates me and I'm grateful to my hubby for organising everything.

In Vietnam, we had the privilege of meeting some amazing people who are responsible for providing the money to educate the country's children. There is no law, no inclination on the part of the government to take responsibility and put education up there as a priority, and sometimes, people just don't have enough money to send their children to school.

The people that we met in Vietnam spent every penny they could on education to improve their children's lives. This gave me two reasons to be grateful: I was thankful for this eye-opening experience, and for the education system that is open to all children in the UK.

A retired teacher and close friend often regales me with her experiences in the profession when we have a cuppa together. The abuse she endured from both parents and children throughout her career was horrendous: threats of mutilation, being kicked and spat at. Yet she was expected to provide an opportunity for thirty or more kids to read, write, play and explore the world in a safe environment every day, as well as emotional support to mums and dads. How lucky we are that well-educated people choose a career to improve the quality of the lives of so many others, both big and small.

My first teacher taught me many things, but the one that sticks in my mind is not to bite my nails. I remember with gratitude how kind and caring she was, giving me the adult guidance I needed in a safe environment I'd never experienced before.

Going to school was confusing to start with as all I had known up until then was abuse at home. I had no boundaries around intimacy, relationships etc. My teacher guided me in the right direction and prevented me from abusing others, as I didn't know that this wasn't actually normal behaviour. I watched boundaries and rules taught not through violence, but through kindness and assertiveness. I was opened up to a completely safe new world full of caring people, and for that I will be forever grateful.

Reading quickly became a joy to be grateful for as I developed a lifelong love of books. Some of my favourite stories were *Cinderella*, *The Princess and the Pea*, *Hansel and Gretel*, to name but a few. I will always be grateful for my journey into the world of imagination that started when I was four.

Gratitude for family

It may sound funny for me to say I'm grateful for the family I had as a child. I do sometimes wonder why none of my extended family members intervened to help me when I was little, but geographical separation probably played a huge part. Things weren't the same as they are today with all our different methods of communication, so I'm not actually sure they knew what was happening.

My gratitude for my grandad and nan to this day brings tears of joy and love to my eyes. The generosity of the unconditional love that they gave me, looking after me and giving me some of the best days in my childhood, will stay with me forever. I remember the joy of perching on top of my uncles' feet while they waltzed me around my grandparents' flat to great roars of laughter, and the visits to the local ice rink where they both speed-skated over the barrels. I am so proud to say that they were my family. They were protective, supportive and kind, and if you could bottle the feeling that gave me, it would be worth a fortune. For that love, I am forever grateful.

On the day of my nan's funeral, I was grateful that my uncles respected my wishes about who carried her coffin in. This was so important to me. When my grandad left this world, his influence continued to inspire me and encourage me to be a good person. When I need a guiding light, he is still there in my heart. The values my grandparents instilled in me have stood strong throughout my life today. If they wouldn't do something, then I won't either. Wow, what a legacy.

Gratitude for friendship

When I ran away from my father's house in County Durham and fled to London, I kept in touch with one friend from school. She and her family offered to take me on holiday to Scotland, which was amazing. Dipping my toes in the lochs, I loved the amazing beauty of the countryside. But more than anything, I loved the fact that no one in her family was unkind to anyone else. I had never been on a family holiday before, and over forty years later, I still hold the memory of this happy time in my gratitude bank.

Another positive memory of this friendship came from tragedy, when one of the dogs the family had was involved in an accident and was killed by a car. While this was sad for everyone, no one blamed anyone else; there were no repercussions that would have made the situation worse. The level of acceptance and kindness this family showed to each other was an amazing eye opener and a fantastic learning curve for me. I took the love and friendship they taught me and am grateful to be able to use it today in my everyday life.

Gratitude for my husband and children

I could write forever about the reasons my husband and children give me to be grateful. Even though pregnancy wasn't a joy for me, giving birth was horrendous as I was always so tiny, the hospital staff did not treat me too well either and I have the scars to prove it.

Wow, what a privilege it is to be a mum. To be able to give to little people and nurture them as they grow bigger. To witness them go through their own ups and downs while offering them unconditional love. I am grateful to have had the opportunity to test my skills as a mother and develop them as we've gone along, forgiving and accepting each other as we are.

My children have all grown up into kind, thought-ful, caring adults and have given me my new name of Granny. I love the whole process of bringing up children, even though it hasn't always been easy. Children challenge us and help us to become better people, so I have learned a lot from my children and have been able to take these skills into many of my other relationships.

Our children are not our possessions; they are merely on loan to us. I have been lucky enough to have made more than my fair share of withdrawals from my loans, not getting fined for over parenting while allowing my kids to grow and develop into themselves.

TALES FROM THE MEMORY BANK

My first husband gave me hope and support when I became a mother. Even though it didn't work out between us, we brought two beautiful children into the world, which is a blessing to be eternally grateful for.

I am also thankful for the memories of my time with this man. He introduced me to the band Madness and a variety of musical artists on top of the ones I had already discovered, one of my favourites being Ian Dury and the Blockheads. Even when this marriage was going wrong, I was grateful for the insights he gave me into what I didn't want in a relationship and the opportunity to work out what I did want. I am grateful that I had the courage to move on, and he had the courage to recognise that he wasn't happy and end it.

Marriage the second time around has presented me with more obvious reasons to be grateful. That my amazing second husband has built me up from being immature to being a fully functioning adult is nothing short of amazing. He has challenged me when I have needed it and given me love and attention unconditionally. Our beautiful son is a balanced mixture of both of us, another blessing to be grateful for.

My life with my husband has been built on trust. He has always allowed me to be who I am and accepted me with all my hang ups. In turn, I have learned to recognise what is normal and what isn't; how to expect to be treated and how to treat others; that I have a value and am worthy of unconditional love.

As I write these words, they fill my heart with enormous pride and love, but our life together hasn't always been easy. We have worked through some tough times, but now we have got more than thirty years under our belts, and that's a wow. I'm grateful that we have both stuck with it, providing help and support not only to our family, but to others in the community who have become our second family.

Gratitude for my career

If it hadn't been for a trusting community psychiatric nurse, I probably wouldn't be where I am today in my career. She saw something in me that even I didn't know I had, and as a result, I have had the privilege of building a career where I have been able to give back to others and be part of helping them through their journey of change, developing new skills in them and transporting them to a better place, which in turn has helped their families. What a fantastic honour it is to do a job like this.

Throughout my career, I have been grateful to have met some of the most fantastic people. On the whole, they have been grateful too and have said thank you. They have all left me with reflections on my practice and helped my learning as well as my humility. Yes, I'm even grateful for timely reminders that I'm not perfect, especially as I have had many interactions with arrogant people who have forgotten where they have come from. It's never a pleasant encounter, but still, I'm grateful. It makes me all the more determined never to take advantage of others.

TALES FROM THE MEMORY BANK

I remember sitting in a car park, waiting to go and speak to a group of people who regarded me as an inspirational woman. Did I ever think anyone would think this of me? No, I didn't. Does this mean I will leave a legacy, something to be proud of? Perhaps it does, but to this day, I find it hard to see the inspiration in myself. But I'm grateful for this struggle as it means I can identify when others are having the same struggle.

My inability to see my value has given me humility that I hope I never lose. But I gratefully recognise what I have achieved. Some people would not have been able to survive what I have experienced in my life, while I have taken from it the opportunity to share my knowledge of life's damaging encounters to benefit others.

My support group, also known as my recovery family, freely gives me encouragement and understanding, accepting me for who I am while challenging me when required. I am supremely grateful for their unconditional care, tolerance and respect. My first contact with my support group was on 29 August 1986, a day I will never forget and always be grateful for. When I was brought into the fold, I didn't have a clue if I was going to fit in, but I didn't need to worry. With delicate handling, this vulnerable child blossomed. It was like a new birth, with all of the pain that goes with that as well as the miracle.

Many other people are given this same opportunity, but choose not to take it. I am grateful that I was ready. Now, I never blame anyone else for my actions; I am responsible for the choices I make. I have learned new skills that have made me into the person I am today, pursuing a career I love. My children got a new mum and my community gained, too. From running a cub pack to setting up a charity to being the chairperson of the local rugby club, I have felt able to give so much back. I can never be too grateful. Without the help I received, so many people wouldn't have got the help I have subsequently been able to give.

This may sound a bit wonky, but if my early life hadn't been so dysfunctional, I would never have needed to seek help, so wouldn't have become equipped to be who I am today. All the abuse, all the trauma – I wish I hadn't had to experience it, but with gratitude, I now see what it gave me: the opportunity to break the mould and become a kind, caring, empathetic woman, particularly towards those who have suffered as I did, giving them hope that change is possible. They too can have a happy life.

My amazing career has been given to me through trust. It has opened doors for me to meet some of the most special people in the world; not the rich and famous, not the ones you see on the telly, but the men and women who are determined to put right the mistakes of the past through change. By owning their journeys with their families and friends, and making time simply to be, they take risks and become inspirations to others. The very people who challenged my existence from the day I was born have allowed me to grow and given me the opportunity to be the mother, wife and mentor I am now.

As a parent, I have had the amazing task of bringing up three children. They show their love to my hubby and me through wanting to still be around us, even though they are in their thirties and forties. We have frank and honest conversations, and I appreciate that we can do this while respecting each other's views. And more recently, they have enabled me to become a granny. What a privilege. So much to be grateful for, and believe me, I am.

FOUR
Mental Health

Some of us have mental health issues in abundance, others not so much. The reality is that we can all learn to manage our mental health in a way that will allow us to live a happy and fulfilled life. Or we can choose not to.

No way out?

There are expectations in society, the things people expect to see. Everyone has an opinion on what a mum is supposed to be and do, whether a father should always be the provider, the traditional hunter-gatherer role, and the mother the main care giver. The reality is that in my formative years, I never measured up to any societal expectation. No healthy sibling rivalry, best friends, boyfriends and girlfriends who followed me through my life; no regular schooling; no knowing where I would be living from one week to the next, or who I was going to live with.

I didn't fit in any of the boxes society had set out for a child, and the impact could have been disastrous for my mental health. At times, it was. The anxiety of what might happen next plagued me as a child and young adult. Concern based on fear of the known and unknown created a melee of emotions that manifested themselves in a variety of ways.

As a child, it was people pleasing, from keeping the house clean and doing chores on behalf of my siblings, to being extra helpful at school, to never telling anyone the family secrets. Doing well at school was important to me in a world where I got no positive recognition at home, but the pressure I felt never to let anyone down was immense.

I continued to be a people pleaser all the way through my teenage years and early adult life. This was the coping strategy I had established to block out the grim reality of life, to cover up the fact that fear was my constant companion. Fear reminded me of all that was horrible in my world, things that either had happened or were going to happen, or perhaps were even happening at that moment in time.

My constant alertness put a huge strain on my mental health, preventing me from sleeping, increasing my heart rate, lowering my mood and giving me an internal feeling of hopelessness. I never knew when my torment would end, and the fear of more pain, both physical and emotional, led me into suicidal thoughts.

TALES FROM THE MEMORY BANK

I didn't see any other way out. It was death or a continuation of my current situation. What a dilemma for anyone to have, especially a young person without the freedom and life skills to look for another option. Could I take my own life? Could I continue to tolerate the abuse?

While the physical pain I endured affected me badly, the constant waiting, wondering what fresh torment was just around the corner, was worse. The what-and-when questions diminished any small glimmer of hope. How was I going to get out of the horror of it all?

This is still a thought process I automatically resort to when I feel overwhelmed, it became so ingrained when I was young. But back then, in a sense, suicide became my friend. It gave me a choice. It gave me an opportunity to escape.

Thankfully, I never followed my suicidal thoughts through. Instead, I fled to London to escape my father's abuse, but the shocking reality was the only thing that really changed was my locality.

The known vs the unknown

When I moved to London, my whole life was turned upside down. While living with my father had had a hugely detrimental effect on my mental health, fear of the unknown was even worse. At least before, I could predict what was coming next.

TALES FROM THE MEMORY BANK

Although a monster in more ways than one, my father was fairly predictable. If he lost while gambling, he would be more violent, or worse, more likely to pay a visit to my bedroom, than if he won. I did everything to avoid him or, if that was impossible, please him to try to mitigate the risk of violence. If I pleased him, he was less likely to be aggressive or disturb me in the night, allowing me at least some hope of sleeping in peace.

To a certain extent, I could manipulate my father's mood. Sadly, I took this people-pleasing behaviour into my adult life, and it was something I had to change for the sake of my mental health.

Running away to the unknown environment of London left me ill-equipped to manage the pain I was experiencing at home from the continued neglect and abuse. Bullying at school just exacerbated the situation. I didn't have a clue what was going to happen next, which left me with no way of dealing with the mental torture in my head.

I resorted to my established coping strategies, but when I cleaned my mother's house from top to bottom, no one noticed. I went to work to provide for myself when I was thirteen. This offered me at least one safe place – until it wasn't safe anymore.

Even more than I had before, I did my best to become invisible. The pressure I put upon myself not to fail, or I would stand out even more than I did already, while working to provide food and clothing for myself was not easy to deal with at thirteen.

Truancy, self-harm and drugs

I had never had to cope with the type of bullying I was experiencing at school in London. It was daily torture from my fellow pupils, constant abuse such as punching, kicking and hateful comments to being completely ignored. As a result, I began to self-harm.

This sadly led me into a new web of deceit. I would harm myself, and then lie about the marks on my body, saying I had fallen over. This, in turn, I used to justify the fact that more and more, I wasn't attending school.

I continued with my self-harm until I discovered mood-altering chemicals. Most of the money I earned was spent on clothes, food and music, but whatever was left over went on drugs to block my constant stream of unwelcome emotions. I hadn't developed the life skills to deal with them in a way that wouldn't compromise my fragile mental health, so I obliterated them with whatever substance I could get my hands on.

TALES FROM THE MEMORY BANK

In my teens, I didn't have a clue that I was dealing with what is now known as post-traumatic stress disorder (PTSD). Back then, mental health was not something we discussed openly, so I was left alone to deal with my current set of traumas as well as I could. As a result, my life spiralled out of control. Internally, I was a frightened teenager with no understanding of the fact that I was unwell. Even if the opportunity had been available to seek help, back then, I was a private person and preferred to keep my emotional insecurities to myself.

After nearly two years of truancy without getting caught, I was found out. Ironically, at the time, I was in hospital and had a valid reason to not be at school. As a result, I was seen by a social worker at school who, quite frankly, did nothing to help me. Our time together was spent talking about her and her newborn child, who she brought along to the session and paid far more attention to than the confused and frightened teenager she was supposed to support.

To this day, I wonder how different my life would have been if just one person had cared enough to find out the reasons behind my truancy. Why would I as a thirteen-year-old girl start failing to attend school when my former school records must have said that was out of character for me? Why wasn't I keeping up with my schoolwork when before, I had been a model pupil? Why I was I so dangerously underweight? Why was I constantly covered in bumps and bruises?

TALES FROM THE MEMORY BANK

Later on in my teens, my addiction to drugs stopped and started depending on whether I was pregnant or not. Thank goodness I was unable to use anything when pregnant as I vomited from conception to birth, which kept my precious load safe.

Nothing stopped the internal torture I had in my head, though, my fragile confidence damaged further by judgemental midwives and doctors. There was little or no care and understanding. No one asked about my wellbeing, even though I lost weight during pregnancy yet had the most enormous bump. After being left in labour for four days, I gave birth to a large baby and was simply told to get on with it. I had so many stitches, I was unable to go to the loo.

All this did was reaffirm to me that this was how I deserved to be treated. Again, abuse and neglect were my normal.

Although I was in constant conflict with my mental health, I never shared my inner turmoil with anyone. My first husband didn't have a clue. I had been conditioned not to reveal anything to anyone, whatever the circumstances. The secrets of my childhood were to be tucked away in the mind chest with the biggest lock you can imagine, and I did the same with my emotions.

I was twenty-four before I realised this was no way to carry on. Can you imagine what the strain of holding all of that torment in had done to my mental health? It's little wonder I hid behind a drug-induced haze.

TALES FROM THE MEMORY BANK

Sadly, I had easy access to drugs: my mother. She was taking a vast number of pills, and I helped myself to them liberally. I regularly overdosed, but by some miracle, I managed to survive.

I didn't want my life to continue. I wanted to end the internal torture, stop the constant worrying about how I would cope. The shame, the loneliness, the inability to manage my emotions – it was getting harder, and I truly thought my children would be better off without me.

I now know that's not true. I survived, I am still here, but it was pure fluke. Occasionally, my thinking still strays towards ending it all. It's a negative coping strategy that I adopted when I was young and in turmoil, but it has never really gone away. I can assure you, I have no intention of ever acting on it;

I recognise I have too much to lose, so challenge myself. But boy oh boy, I wish I didn't think that way. It's a sad legacy of my past substance abuse, and a warning to all of the long-term effects of drugs.

Coping and blocking strategies

It's quite clear to me now that when I was young, I was not healthy mentally. After my divorce, I was left with little or no self-preservation or respect. I had never been taught to respect myself, so how would I know how to do so?

Mood-altering chemicals weren't my only emotion-blocking technique. I also immersed myself in one unhealthy relationship after another. This was my norm until I was educated otherwise.

My anxiety drained me and I was constantly looking for ways to make myself feel better, but nothing seemed to work. I was a parent responsible for two young children while struggling to be responsible about my own mental health. I didn't take into consideration that my life, both past and present, wasn't good because I simply didn't know.

My dysfunctional thinking all became too enormous and I could see no light at the end of the tunnel. I just didn't think I could cope, and the reality was that I couldn't. I tried, but it was to the detriment of my mental health. I worked when I could, I kept house for my mother and her husband, took my kids to school and kept abreast of everything practical – after all, this was familiar. This was what I had been used to all my life, what I had been conditioned to do from an early age. The practicalities of life weren't difficult for me; what was difficult was the constant loneliness.

Whoever I was with, I felt lonely. The enormous dark lump in my tummy never went away. It sat like a heavy meal and I carried it around like a pregnancy with little chance of reaching full term. It seemed the only way out was dying.

In effect, my whole world was my blocking technique. My negative coping strategies mixed in with the trauma of responsibility left me with massive feelings of failure and grief along with scars, both physical and mental. I craved an escape from it all, but all I did was sink further and further into a mire that swallowed me up and would not allow me to change.

My shame around what had happened to me was blocking me from moving on, but I was unaware that this was the case. I absorbed and carried every emotion in my environment, whether it was mine or not. This was a habit I had become an expert on for self-preservation, but it was proving difficult to let go. The temperature of the emotions in my environment would change and I would change accordingly. I spent my life like a protective chameleon, finding new colours to match whatever the mood was around me.

I always tried to make things better, to reduce the conflict. I would wash, cook, clean, give everything I earned through fear, which left me destitute. I would starve myself, which became a mood-altering strategy for me. Sadly, no one noticed when I became a walking skeleton, convincing me further that no one cared and I was so insignificant, I wasn't worth caring for.

TALE FROM THE MEMORY BANK

After my father was convicted for GBH inflicted on a family member, unbelievably, a judge still regarded him as a suitable carer for his children. Suffering from the trauma of overhearing the assault he committed, I was sent back to live with the perpetrator of the crime. I can still remember the horror of literally trembling in the courtroom, waiting for my father to come and get me, and feeling powerless to reverse this travesty of justice. It's a vivid memory that I wish would disappear, but it never has and I doubt it ever will.

My mother came to visit while the court case was taking place. It was the first time I had seen her since she'd left, but still I hoped she had come to rescue me from the violence and abuse that I endured. After taking us for a meal, she then promptly walked out on my siblings and me again. Yes, we were left once again with a man who had proved he wasn't fit to be called a decent human being, let alone a responsible father. This was just one in a seemingly endless stream of events that made me question my worth and value.

Ignorance is bliss, so the saying goes, and when I look back, I recognise that my lack of knowing that my world was completely abnormal was another way for me to block my emotions. Like most of my blocking techniques, though, this was to the detriment of my mental health. Regarding myself as worthless, I was never going to learn to respect and value myself.

I regularly see people suffering from a similar lack of self-regard in my work today, and thanks to my past, I can understand and empathise with how they feel. If you are not given any respect in your formative years, then how the hell are you going to learn how to give it to yourself?

Today, I still have blocks. While generally these blocks revolve around being in denial of my needs and feeling embarrassed to ask for help, rather than feeling I have no worth and trying to hide my emotions behind a screen of self-harm and drugs, I push through. By always looking after my basic needs, I will ensure that my mental health stays healthy, even if it's merely cheering myself up by watching a Disney movie. I now say what I want and need – well, most of the time, anyway.

Some emotions aren't good for me, and I do still have blocking techniques for them, but none that risk harm to my mental health. I know how fragile and precious that is. Shame is one such emotion. It takes me back to a place in time that I have no desire to revisit. While this shame does serve to keep my morals and self-reliance strong, I never want to be overwhelmed by it again as I was as a child. When I feel that happening, my blocking technique is to read, pray and take time to reflect.

I like the fact that my mental health is now so good, I can give back to others, be a good mum, wife and friend. While I don't always get it right, it helps to maintain my mind, body and self-esteem. Completing a neat circle, my mental health then stays in a good place. When times of trauma arise, and they do, I remind myself that I have the choice to restore my mental health. I just need to be who I need to be and continue my journey.

Regular therapy has worked well in keeping my mental health on track, so I would recommend that to anyone who is struggling. The opportunity to share your innermost thoughts and feelings and be validated by another human being gives you a different perspective and allows you the space to get away from any negative emotions that are overwhelming you, finding new options. It's a great way of moving on, as looking after mental health is a key part of being a fully functioning adult.

FIVE
Positive Emotions

Positive emotions, such as love and humility, give me the courage to be who I want to be. But the importance of being true to who you really are can easily be dismissed and swept under the carpet, and I have seen many a good person fail through living a lie. Being and accepting who you are, warts and all, gives you the self-love and the humility to just be.

Humility in the home environment

Ah, humility, something that was sadly lacking in my childhood. My father saw himself as all powerful and used his manipulative skills to convince other adults of this. With me, he used fear, but the implication was always that he was right. What a confusing message to be brought up with – violence and terror left me traumatised, yet I was supposed to believe the perpetrator was in the right.

My father genuinely believed he had the right to help himself to whatever he wanted, forcing a little girl to do things no child should ever have to face, letting her believe the world would be disappointed if she didn't comply. He even forced me to reveal where I was living after the police had advised me not to let him know. How confusing for a child, to be ordered to go against the law. He never worked out that his behaviour was cruel or recognised he was bad, the one in the wrong. Even after going to prison for sexually abusing a young woman (I don't mean me – he never paid for his crimes against me), he still didn't have the humility to admit his faults.

Strangely, right up to his death, there were others who believed him to be a good person, despite evidence to the contrary. That's how manipulative he was. It astounds me that this was a man considered fit to bring up children.

TALES FROM THE MEMORY BANK

My father wasn't the only person in the living environments of my past who was sadly lacking in humility. When I first decided to get clean, the man who ran the rehab facility held a lot of power over the people in his care, and he loved nothing more than to shame them, leaving a trail of destruction rather than healing. He would sit behind his big desk, making sure everyone knew he was the boss and believing he knew best.

This man, who was meant to be providing care, lacked the humility to show any empathy whatsoever. He would throw vulnerable people on the street without any regards for their safety, unless of course they were women and he was attracted to them. Then he could be nice, as he could to people who had money. I didn't fall into either category, so avoided him as much as I could.

I remember someone saying he'd be an angel if he just remembered to attach his wings and act accordingly. Many years later, when I was in a much stronger state of mind myself, I attended a meeting that he was at. By then, he had little to offer and was scrambling around for work, but he still had no humility towards others and their plight. He was as judgemental as ever. What a shame he had learned nothing.

My own learning from this man's lack of humility is always to treat people with equal kindness, whoever they are. In my work, I sometimes have to make hard decisions, but I do my best to make my decisions fair, going to the lengths of checking them out with my team and other clients to ensure I'm on the right path. This not only means I can treat everyone with the respect they deserve, it also keeps me in my place and safe from myself.

Humility in the school environment

For me, school was an environment where humility was either in abundance or not apparent at all. I met some kind, thoughtful people who went beyond the course of duty, and without their help, I'm not sure I would have survived. I also met some who preferred to turn a blind eye to the obvious.

TALES FROM THE MEMORY BANK

One teacher at the last school I attended was outstandingly kind. He could see I was having a hard time and always took the trouble to make sure I was OK, whereas other teachers never seemed bothered about the fact I became pregnant at sixteen. When I asked for help, they told me they were too busy, but I knew the truth was they were not interested enough to involve themselves in a vulnerable teenager's troubles.

When children grow up into adults, they remember who was kind to them and who was not. Kindness is so important in anyone's world, especially when that person is at their most vulnerable, so I firmly believe that people in any caring position need a measure of humility. And that is what the teacher I remember for his kindness had in spades.

I returned to the same school years later to talk to the kids about teenage pregnancy. While I was there, I met a girl who was obviously in trouble, but her teacher's response was 'Not my problem'. I was shocked that, twenty years on, nothing had changed. Humility, people! It's important.

Lots of young people simply need the opportunity to talk with a person they can trust in a safe environment. If things aren't working, especially where young and/ or vulnerable people are concerned, someone needs to be brave and humble enough to say that it needs to change, and make sure it does. Otherwise, what may seem like nothing to a person in a good place mentally can be devastating to someone else. If vulnerable young people are denied the right to help because certain adults are too arrogant to gather the humility to admit something needs to change, it makes me seethe.

Humility in healthcare

Anyone can do good things for no other reason than because they care, but they need humility, not arrogance. It's a myth that successful people are always arrogant; many people are in top professions because they have the humility to create hope for others.

Healthcare by its very nature is a sector that is full of vulnerable people and those who care for them. There are many highly successful medics who are shining examples of caring, humble professionals. And, of course, human nature being what it is, there are some who aren't.

TALES FROM THE MEMORY BANK

I recently had a breast check – not the most enjoyable experience in the world, but with a little humility on the part of the professionals I encountered, it could have been so much better. Having had to wait over two weeks for an appointment, I was told that all my tests would be done on one day; but they weren't. I was simply told that I had a lump in my breast. This showed a total disregard for my feelings.

At my next appointment, having already experienced the pain of having had a mammogram, which bloomin' hurt, I was waiting naked from the waist up to be seen. A guy walked in and said he was there to scan my breast, offering little in the way of either communication or respect for me or my body.

That day, I learned the lump was a cyst. I had to wait for over two weeks for the result of my scan, although the medic had said he would get back to me in a few days. My family was worried, constantly asking if the results were through yet.

The whole experience made me aware that sometimes people wield power that can make or break someone else's mood, leaving them either worried and distressed or relieved and positive. How wonderful it would be if we all employed some humility and opted for the latter.

Give humility a try

When someone has accumulated wealth, either in knowledge or financially, and they use it to do good by sharing it, this shows they have humility. Even if all we can give is time – time to listen, cut the lawn, drive someone to an appointment, read a book, cook a meal – we can all take a look around us, recognise the needs others have and share whatever we can with them. It all helps, and it makes us appreciate what we have all the more.

Humility gives and doesn't take. It offers kindness and hope, consideration and warmth. It's saying sorry, admitting when you've made a mistake – I have made a lot in more ways than one. It's going beyond the call of duty and never resenting it, giving more than what's expected of you. It's being open about your hopes and dreams, showing that it's OK to fail and pick yourself up. You can be poor financially, yet be rich with life's experiences.

Humility is never too proud to ask for help. It believes that everyone is equal and treats them accordingly, recognising the beauty of others and the world at large. We humans do not hold all the power; there is something greater than ourselves.

Humility is always worth a try in my opinion. It has given me hope, guidance and a life way beyond my wildest dreams. And when it's paired with love, it's a marriage made in heaven.

Feel the love

Allowing love to become a part of myself, bringing with it trust, kindness and hope, has opened me up to the world. In my business, I truly love other people's success and enjoy being a part of their transformation of change. These feelings envelop me. Even when someone has disappointed me with an unkind action or poor choice, I have learned to move on and allow my love to revive itself.

Seeing another succeed in whatever they endeavour to pursue gives me a warm, proud feeling. This capacity to enjoy someone else's success, such as the time one of my closest friends sold his part of a company for a lot of money, makes me feel like my heart will burst. He had put in so many hours, and his effort was now paying him back.

I rejoiced when my son had a record played on the radio; when a guy I'd helped turned his business around after he'd lost a lot; when a friend's son finally got his shit together and became successful in his own right. It's these special moments filled with love that words just cannot describe.

Love means I can push jealousy to one side, allowing the pleasure of hope and recognition to move in. Jealousy can close off a person who has the potential to be kind and generous, while love opens them up so they can strive to achieve in all circumstances. With love for myself, I have worked on not comparing myself to whatever others have achieved, which can often lead to feelings of inadequacy. When I see other charities gain funding where mine hasn't, for example, it could leave me feeling frustrated if I allowed it to eat away at me. Then I would be giving out negative vibes rather than feeling the love.

If I close my heart and mind to the possibilities around me and only look at the 'if only', then my mind and heart don't develop. They are prevented from seeing the world from a different perspective, unwilling to explore new waters. Closure is just that: closed to the possibility of living from a different perspective through love.

To me, love is honesty and honesty is love. When I hold on to the resentments of my past, it blocks my ability to forgive and move to loving again. It has taken many years to develop that side of me and I still have to work at it. It is so easy to detach, but this makes my world smaller than it needs to be. The value is in opening up to share my true feelings, breaking down my defences and allowing myself and all around me to grow.

When you're honest and come from a foundation of love, people will listen. I have found that the power of prayer and meditation helps, options that are always there if I choose to take them.

Love and resentment

It may sound crazy, but love and resentment can go hand in hand. If someone you love treats you badly, then it's easy to hold both negative and positive feelings towards them.

I have found that holding out the hand of love backed up by honesty allows the feelings of resentment to diminish. In my opinion, it doesn't have to go completely; any resentment I feel is part of the learning process I have gone through. It's all part of my education. But if you truly love someone, you wish them no harm and don't think or act negatively towards them, even in anger.

TALES FROM THE MEMORY BANK

I was once accused of being a bad person. The first time I could forgive, but the second time, my bank of emotions checked it out and verified that the accuser was wrong. There was no honesty behind the accusation, so where was the love?

Frankly, honesty and love have to go hand in hand, and for me, that means loving and being honest with myself as well as others. Self-examination allows me to be true to who I am. I have to see the loving, caring person inside me, or I slip far too comfortably into being the terrified people pleaser of my youth. This conditioning from childhood is difficult to break down – the automatic response to my being treated in a way that suggested I was bad, never receiving any affirmation to the contrary. I can honestly say, my father never once told me he loved me.

True love

I've had some amazing love given to me and I've been able to give love in return. The birth of each of my children overwhelmed me in a good way with the immense love that only a parent can relate to. It's a moment that words don't and can't describe: a feeling of love that is so deep, it hurts; of being the protector, provider and parent, and never wanting to let go; of recognising innocence and beauty, combined with the responsibility for what lies ahead.

TALES FROM THE MEMORY BANK

The moment I met my husband, while we were unable to act upon our feelings, the affection we had for each other was instant. We went on to be friends until 1987 when he returned from Africa and asked if we could take the friendship in a different direction. Even though I was in early recovery, we had such strong history, I took the plunge.

At the altar on our wedding day, which we shared with my two children, I felt such an overwhelming surge of love and joy as we knelt and the vicar brought us all together as one family. The vicar who married us said later that it was the happiest wedding he had ever been to. He identified the depth of love that was present not just between us, but also from our friends. We only had a small wedding, yet people turned up from everywhere to watch and greet us in the street outside the church.

Holding a grandchild for the first time, sharing that moment of becoming a parent with your own kids, is another powerful experience. It's a whole different kind of love to becoming a parent yourself. Being included in a part of your own children's journey, and bringing support and reassurance when required, fills your heart. It is surprising how much love you can have for these new little people in your world, while still loving your own children as much as you ever did.

While I was writing this, my heart filled with love for my husband, who has loved all three of my children unconditionally and equally. Even though he isn't the biological father of the older two, you would never know this if you saw him with them, and I adore him for that. Having experienced poor parenting from my own stepparents, I admire and respect the commitment my husband shows.

It was love that made me realise as a child that I wasn't on my own; there is something greater than me to hold me and guide me. I was lonely and scared for most of my childhood, so I loved the fact that I'd found this higher power. It filled my heart and gave me hope that things would get better.

Love means allowing others into your life. Then you are no longer an island. You're on an all-encompassing journey through the world, gathering the joys of love on the way. Love will open you up to truth and honesty. Being kind, thoughtful and caring is all part of love, and when it all comes together, then the rewards are ten-fold.

SIX
Positive Traits

The positive traits you adopt in your life have to be based on your values and beliefs. If you stray from these, you compromise your integrity. This doesn't mean you cannot change your values and beliefs; as you learn and grow throughout life, sometimes it's essential, but always stick to the principles you have set out for yourself. This allows your own personal integrity to stay solid.

Before we have a look at values, let's examine integrity. What is it, who has it and where does it come from?

The integrity of family

Wow, this one's a biggie. I don't think my parents had any integrity whatsoever. My father in particular never established what was right or wrong and how others should be treated.

Having integrity as a family means giving children a solid foundation to grow up to become people any community would be happy and proud to have represent them. And to sustain this even when things are not so good. Oh, how I wish my family had given me this start in life.

Integrity is not something any of us can fake. That would be like attending church every Sunday like a fine upstanding Christian, then going home and bullying your wife, husband or child. Unfortunately, I have witnessed people trying to fake it over and over again in my life.

TALES FROM THE MEMORY BANK

Today, when I was reading my son's Instagram post about mental health and helping others, it made me proud to see how the integrity of the family unit I helped to build is carrying on through our children. Acknowledging that all humans may at some time need support or help, whatever their circumstances, our son has shown that our integrity as a family means we can look out for each other and offer a hand of kindness when it's needed.

My father never showed integrity, never looked beyond his own needs. His own desires always came first. When he wanted food, he had it with no thought for the fact his children were going hungry. On many an occasion, we would be the bystanders, watching him eat while our tummies rumbled. How can anyone do that to a child, or indeed another human being? It is the lack of values, the antithesis of integrity.

When I ran away from home, it was nearly a week before my father contacted the police. He had no idea where my sister and I were or who we were with, yet he didn't think to check we were safe. Once again, he'd failed as a parent. What kind of person would not report their missing children? One without a shred of integrity.

My mother loved to be seen to do things for others, just as long as the world was watching. She applied to a housing association for a flat, saying she needed the space so she could have her children back with her. Yes, this did happen, but then she returned to her alcoholic husband and took us with her. Her actions seemed to go against any sense of integrity a mother should have. Instead of being provided with safety and security, kindness and love, we followed her into a house where addiction brought with it trauma and abuse.

What is integrity?

Liars do not have integrity. If you pass your child's door on the way to see the local vicar, knowing your child needs you but preferring to see and be seen at church, you are living a lie and have no integrity. It's the same if you call your boss, saying you're unwell and can't come to work when you're actually out with your friends. It's the same if you tell your husband or wife you have to work late, when in actual fact you're carrying on with someone else behind their back. I think you get the picture.

When I've had to make tough decisions, especially about my own children, I have stuck to what I believe in, stuck with my integrity. Even though people around me were suggesting my children would be better off if I had them taken into care, I was keeping them with me, no matter what. They were my children and I would fight to the death for them.

One lesson I learned from both my parents' lack of integrity was always to put my children's needs and safety first. My parents' failings made me determined to do my best in my role as a mother, to provide love, protection and guidance to my children. I haven't always got it right, but I can be proud of what I've done as it came from a place of integrity. I had built strong values and my actions reflected these.

Where does integrity come from?

To be honest, mine has come from all the things that people around me did wrong during my formative years, and beyond. I've learned from their mistakes and the feelings their actions left me with. I've learned that integrity lives in the life blood running through my veins whenever I act based on the principles of kindness and love. It's at the core of what makes me want to get up in the morning.

TALES FROM THE MEMORY BANK

From the pleasure I got from the ice cream my grandad bought for me to the constant trauma of the abuse that I suffered daily – the scars both emotional and physical – my past has gone towards building the integrity I have now. Yes, I've made mistakes. I once hit my daughter with a frying pan – not something I'm proud of. I left my kids with my mother and stepfather, the same people with whom I had suffered so much unhappiness and pain, so I had the space to improve myself to become a better person. The reason behind it doesn't make it right, but the shame I now feel for my actions feeds the integrity I have today.

The reality is that I don't want to repeat the poor decisions of my past and leave others feeling abused, aggrieved or dismissed. If I fail to learn from my mistakes, then I'll just be repeating the family patterns, so I make sure I do learn.

I wonder if people are born with integrity and it's the environment we are brought up in that can diminish it over time? Or is it mind over matter? When we make the decision to be true to ourselves, learn what really matters, our mind will surely help us determine the right roadmap to follow in life. Then our integrity can only grow.

Integrity in others

I remember finding my mother in a compromising position with another man when she was married to my father. I didn't understand the implications of what I was seeing at the time, but even then, it felt kind of wrong. I never told anyone for fear of reprisals and the inevitable tornado of destruction they'd bring with them, but it brought to my attention to what you do *not* do in a marriage.

I experienced unfaithfulness in a past relationship, which added the value of faithfulness to my integrity. I love my husband and would never want him to feel what I did; the degradation and humiliation of realising that someone was lying to me and carrying on behind my back took away my trust and faith in relationships. Their lack of integrity had a negative impact on me, but still I used it as an opportunity to learn.

I believe marriage is for life, even though I failed in my first attempt. It would be easy to lay the blame and shame at the feet of my first husband, but who am I to do so? All this does is cause more pain, more questions. And more importantly, it diminishes my integrity.

TALES FROM THE MEMORY BANK

As a young woman, I met someone who I thought was an upstanding and honest person. I truly believed they had integrity, but that turned out not to be the case.

They offered to help with our finances by sorting out a savings policy for myself and my first husband. As it turned out, they worked for a company that basically stole our money. They were more than aware of our status, knew that we didn't have much to our name, yet chose to take every penny.

What would make one human being cause so much misery to another, just to gain a few pounds? A lack of integrity, that's what. This person clearly had no values strong enough to build integrity upon.

I've worked with people who haven't had the same integrity as myself. Does this change the dynamic of the relationship? Yes, it does, but it also makes me challenge my own integrity. Am I right in how I think and respond? This keeps me on my toes and makes sure I respect other people's views.

Funnily enough, the people I work with now often say that if I wouldn't do something, they won't either. While this makes me smile, it sometimes makes me wonder if I'm being arrogant or hierarchical. This questioning of my own actions makes me open about my integrity and where it has come from. What is right and what is wrong? Just because something is my opinion, it doesn't make it right for everyone; it just makes me who I am. Without our own strong integrity, we all run the risk of getting left behind by our friends, colleagues and community.

TALES FROM THE MEMORY BANK

I was a trustee for a famous charity, but sadly I felt I had to step down after I was accused of being unkind to someone on the phone. This challenged my integrity and left me devastated.

This upsetting experience made me realise that other people don't always have the same integrity as I do. If I stick to my own values and express my integrity honestly, they may feel threatened by it. When others avoid accountability for their own conduct, it is often at the expense of good people.

When an organisation is wrapped up in itself, failing to recognise that change needs to occur, the people within it can become pack animals when someone questions the core of their day-to-day actions. Sadly, this still goes on. Many an organisation fails to make itself and its leaders accountable for their actions, and as a result, often the people it's supposed to be serving are denied the level of service they have every right to expect. Once an organisation has lost its integrity, it has little left to offer.

While it hurt to walk away from something I once believed in, it has given me insight and learning to improve my own integrity. I now trust my instinct far more readily than I used to. When something doesn't feel right, someone's actions don't sit well with me, then it generally transpires that their integrity and mine aren't in the same league. I won't allow my own integrity to be shadowed by that of other people. I won't allow my integrity to be damaged by association.

Having looked at what integrity is, we can now take a look at what it must always have behind it: solid values. Values are linked with integrity, highlighting the attitude and responses we show to the world and their impact on others.

Values deserve respect

I had a bad experience with a waitress who was so insensitive towards the values I hold for myself, she didn't even bother to find out if there was alcohol in a dish she was serving. Despite me making it clear that I have chosen not to touch alcohol for over thirty years, she still brought over a dish that was steeped in rum. What part of serving alcohol to someone who has chosen to be teetotal did she think was OK?

People's values are important to them, so we need to respect them. We can also expect others to respect our values. No one has the right to force their beliefs on to anyone else. No one has the right to dismiss someone else's values. Values are hugely important, not there to be diminished or regarded as insignificant. If ever someone does dismiss your values, you have every right to make your feelings known respectfully and clearly.

TALES FROM THE MEMORY BANK

There will always be people who don't appear to value those around them at all, which brings into question whether they have even considered their own personal values. When entering a shop, for example, I expect to be treated with respect and politeness, but a recent experience in a ladies' wear shop certainly didn't live up to my values.

From the moment I stepped through the door, the owner offered me nothing but arrogance and poor customer service. Yes, I could make excuses for her; perhaps she was having a bad day, but she was rude and unkind, and to this day, I have never gone back to the shop.

The learning I took from this is to treat everyone as a human being and not a commodity. I can afford to spend my money in this shop as much as the next person, but I have to be true to my values, and I value good customer service. That doesn't include a shop owner openly judging me and finding me lacking.

Yes, it's important to respect other people's values, but if they don't respect mine, the deal is off.

Values at work

My values highlight the enormous responsibility that I hold in the counselling room. Someone's life can be changed one way or another by a counsellor, and if the listener is inattentive, this is incredibly disrespectful to the speaker.

We're all human, though, and sometimes our minds will wander. If I haven't heard what a client has said, I just say so and ask them to repeat it. My values and integrity lead me to make sure I have heard and understood everything a client wishes to share with me.

TALES FROM THE MEMORY BANK

A client I had worked with many years ago contacted me as he felt he needed some more time with me. While I am rubbish at remembering names, he was amazed how much I remembered about our sessions together. How could I recall his back story after all this time? Because I cared enough to listen and understand the first time around. And no, I didn't read the notes I'd made then as they had been destroyed.

I pride myself on being able to recall everything a client has told me, even if their name has slipped away into the recesses of my mind. If they have trusted me enough to share their innermost thoughts with me, I value that trust. My professional values ensure that trust is the backbone to everything I do.

Valuing myself and others gives me a sense of responsibility to bring kindness, love and consistency into my clients' worlds. My honesty allows freedom of thought and emotion to all parties. If I can be open about my own values, then my clients feel that they can, too.

TALES FROM THE MEMORY BANK

Once, an ex-client who I had asked for payment accused me of being all about money – which is not a value I hold, and I hope I never will. I love giving to others, but I do believe that people have a right to see a monetary value in whatever they do for a living. The rent or mortgage has to be paid. There is a bigger picture every time.

Whatever our values, we all need to work for our money, so to a certain extent, I am doing it for the money. But that is based on the value of giving back. I earn a living, which means I don't rely on the government or anyone else to prop me up, leaving the benefits system open to those who truly need it.

While recognising and respecting the values others hold, I never feel I have to adopt those values, too.

Their values are their choices, and we all make choices that are personal to us. But I love others sharing their different opinions with me as it opens my world in a positive way, allowing diversity to come through into my life. This then gives me the option to adapt and change my values and beliefs, if I choose to do so.

Values in the home

When I was young, I honestly believed that the value of a child was to slave for their parents. My whole childhood was spent serving my parents, through either chores or sexual gratification. Recognising that this was actually as far from the purpose of a child as it's possible to get came as a revelation to me in many ways.

TALES FROM THE MEMORY BANK

The first intimation I had that there was something very wrong with the family values I held as normal was when I noticed my grandparents didn't treat my uncles in this way. I knew that my uncles were their children, so it was strange to me to see my grandparents speak kindly to them and appreciate them.

Thank goodness, this gave me some insight into how family members should value each other. My own kids would moan about me making them do chores around the house, which would make me laugh; rather than treating them like slaves, as I had been, I was equipping them with the values and skills to run a home of their own when they reached adulthood. Hopefully, they will do the same with their own children.

I'm proud that my children all grew up able to cook, clean and keep a nice home. It is lovely to share a meal with them in a safe and caring environment, and know I have been part of instilling those values in them.

Values in friendship

Although values are personal, it's important when you're choosing your friends that you find people who share your values. Otherwise, you can find yourself left exhausted and feeling more than a little taken advantage of.

With people who share the same values, friendship becomes unconditional. My friends and I don't do things for each other for recognition; we do them because we can. I value the gifts I have been given and like to share them to help others either change their lives or accept what they have, which on reflection is another kind of change. (I'm laughing as I write this.)

TALES FROM THE MEMORY BANK

Someone once said I don't forgive, which is strange because I do. I'm very forgiving, but there are some people I just don't want to forgive. And that is my prerogative, so I need to give myself permission to choose based on my own values.

I struggle to forgive those who are unkind to others. I certainly struggle to forgive those who do things that affect my family directly. When someone decided to steal something that I'd worked hard to establish, I chose not to forgive them based on my values. In fact, I would like to take revenge on this person, but my values won't allow me to do this.

What I have had to accept is that my friends continued to socialise with the person who wronged me. Their values are for them to decide, not for me. It doesn't devalue our friendship, even though deep down, it bloody hurts.

Value your own values, and respect those of others. The way you live your life and the values you hold dear are entirely up to you – unless, of course, they affect someone else.

I'm in the business of encouraging people to challenge their values and choices. This doesn't mean I think mine are right and theirs are wrong; I'm continually challenging my own values, too, and what works for me today may be obsolete tomorrow. I don't agree with everything my children and their children get up to, but I respect the fact it's their choice based on their own values. It doesn't stop me from asking questions and saying what I feel, which satisfies an important part of my integrity, values and beliefs. It also gives them the right to question me, too. Mutual respect for each other's values and right to choose those values, while recognising the right of anyone to question those values if they regard their impact as negative, brings people together.

SEVEN
Self-reliance

When I was in treatment, I often saw those around me making poor choices. Casual sexual relationships and mood-altering chemicals do nothing for vulnerable people apart from temporarily dulling their feelings in the moment. What they fail to do is sustain the change these people need to make in their lives – the very reason they decided to attend treatment in the first place. Tragically, two of the people I am thinking about are in their graves because they didn't stick to their rehab roadmap.

When I first left rehab, I was so insecure; I became hooked on finding comfort in casual sexual relationships. I quickly realised my mistake – how could someone I treated so casually have my best interests at heart? It's dependency at its worse because the so-called remedy is not a drug, but another human being, bringing all their issues and insecurities into the mix.

We can regard dependency on someone or something other than ourselves as being like eating an unbalanced diet. If we don't get the right measure of protein or carbohydrates or vitamins or fat, our body won't function correctly and we end up becoming unwell. If we get the wrong mix of stimulation when our mind isn't healthy, it leads to us adopting poor coping strategies. Although I didn't immediately realise it, I was pretty unwell when I left rehab. I needed to work on my self-reliance rather than expecting a man, drug or drink to change my feelings.

Self-reliance prevents neediness. It allows independent feelings and lack of conformity to shine through, enabling us to build our values, which bring with them self-esteem and a sense of pride and ownership.

But there is a caveat: you can be too self-reliant, which can exclude you from relationships. It can breed a level of arrogance and a lack of empathy. I have to admit that I speak from experience: if I'm not careful, I can become too self-reliant and it isn't pretty. I can literally switch off from others, and while this prevents me from continuing in a situation that is detrimental to me, it can also make me a little judgemental.

I need self-reliance to sustain my current level of professionalism, as well as a healthy family life. A good balance between giving and receiving allows my self-reliance to flourish. When things are not as they should be with one person, then I use my ability to detach positively. Going within myself, I find the armour I require to move on and be there for the next person. Why would I invest in someone who doesn't want my investment?

Delayed gratification

When we seek instant gratification, it can become a kind of spiritual blocking that fails to take the 360° view. It doesn't allow learning through the pain of not getting what we want when we want it. How can we develop if we are unwilling to wait and see, to allow our emotions to progress and to hone the relevant skills to make and enjoy pure choices? If we trap our emotions by fixating on something outside of ourselves, then we are less likely to become a fully functioning adult. This can lead to negative coping strategies, such as self-harm.

I love the seven stages of development Carl Rogers describes in his book *On Becoming a Person*.[2] This brings clarity to the process of change, recognising that it bounces backwards and forwards.

---

2   C Rogers *On Becoming a Person: A therapist's view of psychotherapy* (Robinson, 1977)

If you keep an open mind, then change will occur. If you try to fix yourself using outside sources, then it won't. By dulling your emotions artificially, you inhibit your internal development. It's like making a fresh cheese and hoping it will have the same flavour of a mature batch. Just like the cheese, your emotions need to sit and rest for a while, allowing the flavours to mature. It takes time, and if you cut into your cheese too soon, it can be a disappointment.

Delayed gratification means you're not scooping off all the best parts of life before you are ready to look after them and mould them into a whole being. Instant gratification is like eating your favourite parts of the cake and leaving the other bits. Cake is meant to be enjoyed as a whole, and if you exclude any part of it, then it isn't cake. Enjoy the whole journey of change, the good, bad and indifferent.

TALES FROM THE MEMORY BANK

I use a lot of third eye work with my clients, looking on a situation from the perspective of the outside world. While they look down on to their life from this perspective, I ask them if it is the way they want it to be.

I love doing this work with the people I see professionally, allowing them to see the reality of a situation before they were part of it while exploring it as it is today. It shows how their situation could be seen by others, as well as my own interpretation and that of the client. Even little people get this.

Third eye work and its effect on the client reminds me of an architect drawing up the plans for a new home. They come up with the basic idea, but you have the choice to decide whether they have represented what you want and where you would like it to change, who you want to build it and paint it, and who will live in it.

Leaving poor choices behind

If we don't take a journey away from the poor choices of our past, then it's like building a new home on quicksand rather than solid concrete foundations. No one in their right mind would pick the former, so why do so many of us go for what looks pretty and makes us feel good in the short term rather than exploring the options?

If you build your life on quicksand, it is more than likely to collapse around you. If it's built on the rock, then the chances are it will survive longer. You could look at it as going from the conscious self to a deeper level of understanding. We can all be distracted by the things around us that have tempted us in the past, if we don't allow ourselves to leave the bad choices we've made behind and grow. Having been through this journey of change myself and recognising the benefits it leads to, despite the road sometimes being the more difficult and less trodden one, I will go to any length to help others develop, supporting them in positive personal and professional change.

TALES FROM THE MEMORY BANK

When I first went into business with a partner, I noticed my true self was becoming diminished by their values. They considered it strange when I wanted to support a vulnerable adult by taking them to the doctor to get them checked out. Just because someone shows the hand of kindness, it doesn't make them odd; it just makes them kind.

If I had encountered this attitude in my youth, my people-pleasing coping strategy would have come into effect and I would have changed my values simply to meet my former business partner's. The vulnerable person would then have been denied the help they so clearly needed – not a good outcome for anyone.

Happily, as I had been on my own tough journey of change and had come out the other side with my values and integrity firmly in place, I was able to question my business partner's values and realise that they weren't coming from the same place as I was. They didn't have an open mind, and their coping strategy of mistrust was preventing their growth.

Therapy and self-examination allow us to grow within. Without this growth, we remain the same person with the same responses. We never change, never develop and never leave our poor choices where they belong: in the past.

My journey to self-reliance

If I had stayed with my family when I was young, hoping for a different outcome, I would have been deluding myself and letting my children down. I would have spent my entire life hiding behind my coping strategy, trying to put right other people's actions and reactions, never realising that the only actions and reactions I can take responsibility for are my own.

TALES FROM THE MEMORY BANK

My stepfather had little tolerance and most people tiptoed around him, hoping to pacify him. This included my mother, my children, my husband, the congregation at the church we all attended – I could go on. But it didn't matter what we did, because he never took a good look at himself. Instead of taking responsibility for his own shortcomings, he blamed other people for them, and as the people pleaser I was, I saw nothing wrong with this.

He could be rude at times, to the point of being unkind. He would put people down, and then claim he was only joking if someone did have the guts to challenge him. The mistake I made for many years was not challenging his actions, thereby playing my part in allowing his conduct to carry on. My need for recognition, to be loved and cared for, left me exposing myself and my children to his behaviour.

I needed to change this. I needed to become self-reliant and break away from my constant search for validation from others, which meant I had to go through the pain of not having a parental figure around me anymore. This choice eventually paid off. I no longer had to pussyfoot around this bully of a man and my children no longer had the emotional upset of dealing with his put downs. We had the freedom to become our true selves. This self-reliant change made me a stronger, more congruent individual.

Before I had gone through my journey to become my true self, I did sometimes challenge the behaviour of those around me, but I did it fearfully. Unsurprisingly, even though my challenge did usually bring about some change in the individual I had challenged, it was only ever temporary. Then their behaviour went back to the way it had always been.

Change has to come from within, and only you can decide to make the change, leave your coping strategies and bad decisions behind you, and grow into your true self. I warn you now, there isn't an instant fix. It's like losing weight: it's hard work and it takes time, but when you get there, the rewards you reap are so worth the effort you have put in.

TALES FROM THE MEMORY BANK

Many years after I had made the decision to leave my sorry past behind and grow into the person I wanted to be, a person who could make good and healthy decisions based on values and integrity that would benefit both myself and those I love, my daughter challenged me when I was about to send yet another dutiful card to my mother. My mother had moved away, and even though I wrote to her every week, nothing came back. When my daughter asked why I bothered, I realised she was right.

There but for the grace. If only I had realised earlier in my life how good it felt to free myself from the shackles of duty towards those who I considered deserved nothing from me, I would have done it all the sooner. Stepping back gave me the gratification of being able to choose who deserves to be in my family and who doesn't.

Being clear about what and who you are allows you to be open minded and accept that the choices you make, if they're based on your integrity and values, are built on firm foundations. I discovered that I could thrive on my own without constantly seeking the so-called support of my dysfunctional family. I alone am enough. I don't need recognition from anyone else.

I can't change another person's opinion or action, but neither do I have to accept it. Now, I take responsibility only for my own opinions and actions. If something feels right, it is, and if it doesn't, then it isn't.

Self-development

For me, self-reliance and resilience come as natural by-products of self-development. Without this, I would have been unable to work on my resilience.

TALES FROM THE MEMORY BANK

Through self-development, I have learned to recognise the reality behind what I may regard as my faults. When I am judgemental, for example, then it generally means that something in the person I'm judging has impacted negatively on me. I'm not excusing my faults, just helping my self-development by recognising the reasons behind them and learning from those reasons.

In London, I was aware that there were people living nearby who were culturally different to me. While insisting on arranging what they considered a good marriage for their daughters, some men in certain cultures would disrespect other people's daughters, trying to get sexual favours from them. This tested my values, giving birth to prejudices that I was unaware were impacting on my day-to-day life. Being prejudiced goes completely against my values.

Through self-development, I was able to put my judgemental feelings to one side. I don't want prejudice to hinder my work with people from any culture, so self-exploration still features in my continual self-development. I have learned to respect both myself and others as a result, thank goodness.

There are unfortunately people I have encountered in my profession who have neglected their own self-development, leading them to exploit vulnerable individuals through their work, taking advantage of them and crossing ethical boundaries. These boundaries are put in place for a reason: to provide safety for people who are looking for help and support.

TALES FROM THE MEMORY BANK

The first time I went to seek professional help in my younger days, I explained the reason I needed to talk, which was to explore my feelings towards the appalling things I had suffered as a child. The mental health worker started making jokes about sexual abuse. This shocked me to the core and has stuck with me.

Since I've become a counsellor/therapist myself, I have realised from this experience that it's important to explore your own issues before you are able to conduct yourself appropriately around the people you are meant to be helping.

I later went to work with this person and when I witnessed their behaviour towards vulnerable people, I realised they hadn't progressed.

It took a serious incident for this person to be 'moved on', but this obviously didn't address the underlying problem: it would have been good practice to deal with it head on and ensure this person got the training they needed to develop into an empathetic professional.

This experience did have one positive for my own self-development: I became determined never to accept bad practice.

It is a real bugbear for me when professionals don't report other professionals for misconduct. Why is this? Is it some weird misguided loyalty? Believe me, it's the vulnerable people to whom unprofessional professionals are doing untold damage who deserve that loyalty, not those who don't recognise or accept that they need to work on their self-development. I always follow the path I know to be right, living up to my values by challenging the behaviour of others, including myself. If I feel I need self-development, I make sure I get it.

The day I fail to do the right thing by the people I strive to help is the day I need to stop doing what I do. The ethical boundaries in my profession must stay strong. If someone takes up a position of care and responsibility, they have in effect made a promise to vulnerable people. If they then cross the boundaries, it brings into question the integrity of the entire profession.

Resilience

Developing and sustaining a relationship with ourselves and others requires a level of resilience. When we let ourselves and other people down, it tends to mean there's not enough resilience built into the relationship.

When the people around me have let themselves down through their actions, I have chosen to deal with it to the best of my ability. This builds resilience within myself as well as the relationship I have with the other person. Resilience and tolerance go hand in hand.

TALES FROM THE MEMORY BANK

The times in my past when I have woken from my suicide attempts have shown me that I am meant to live and make the most of it. When the pain of my life left me emotionally exhausted, unable to explore the past, present or future, hope seemed a dim and distant prospect. I was unable to change what had happened, was happening and what would surely happen again. Suicide seemed like an option, one that I clung on to for a while, but for whatever reason, I never succeeded in following it through.

Then I knew I needed to make changes. I had to build the resilience to live. I had to trust that I could change my circumstances and learn to forgive myself.

Financial security was something we never had when I was a young child. The TV and furniture were often repossessed the moment they were brought into the house, and we regularly had to move because the rent wasn't paid. For this reason, financial security has always been important to me as an adult.

To build something that would allow me to pay the bills and still have money left over at the end of the month takes resilience. What I have learned is this comes with time and patience. Hard work, spending wisely and sharing what I have to give, be it a counselling session or buying a raffle ticket from a local group that supports young people with learning difficulties, all helps to build my resilience. Those who hold on to their money, who don't invest in their communities, fail to recognise the importance of them. If and when their resilience lets them down and they need the support of their community, it won't be there. Self-reliance is great to have, but we all could face times when we need the support of others, and this need shouldn't be ignored. Look after your local community to build the foundations for the future.

Resilience has helped me health-wise, too. I have to have one of the worst track records I know for ill health, which has made me realise it's up to me to build my own resilience and manage whatever comes my way. This demonstrates courage and models a way of living rather than just existing. Of course, I thank those who continually support me, especially my husband who must have been an angel sent from heaven to have promised to be by my side in sickness and health. But ultimately, it is my self-reliance and the resilience that has enabled me to build that has seen me through.

EIGHT
Negative Emotions

When something is put under pressure, such as an elastic band being extended to its full length, it's likely to cause pain somewhere along the line. If whoever is holding the other end lets go, it is going to snap back at you and that will hurt. If you let go first, it will hurt them. Alternatively, the pressure on its elasticity will become too much and it will snap, which isn't a great outcome for the rubber band.

Stress

We're all susceptible to stress. A baby crying for its milk feels the stress of hunger. An elderly person needing the bathroom in the middle of the night feels the stress of a full bladder and broken sleep. Stress is a normal emotion which is there for a reason. The reasons are not necessarily clear at the beginning of our journey, but if we keep our eyes and minds open, then the chances are enlightenment will come.

I don't really do stress. Or rather, I don't let stress dictate to me how I feel. I do 'Let's find a resolution' rather than seeing it as hard work, worry or too much contemplation. Sadly, I have witnessed the negative impact of stress on a lot of people. This not only affects them health-wise, it also affects their psychological attitudes and those of the people around them. Think of employees who ruin their colleagues' day because they allow stress to take control of their mood and responses.

TALES FROM THE MEMORY BANK

I sometimes wonder if people use stress as an excuse for their bad behaviour. When I was young, other people's stress, or rather the foul mood they allowed stress to put them into, left me on tenterhooks, wondering what was going to happen next. I remember being in a car with a driver who descended into road rage. I was terrified, which resulted in me jumping out of a moving car to get away from them.

The driver later apologised, saying they were under a lot of stress. That was their excuse, anyway, but what right did they have to make me feel so frightened?

It all comes back to choices. The reality is, if we think about things rationally, then there is often nothing to be stressed about. We all need to stop pulling on the elastic band and realise that stressing is getting us nowhere. At its worst, it can be making our lives miserable, which impacts on those we care about and those around us, when the pain is in fact self-inflicted. We have choices in how we deal with stress; we just have to decide which one we take.

We also have choices in how we deal with another negative emotion that often eats away at us, sometimes without us realising it. That emotion is shame.

The shame of my childhood

My sad truth is that shame was such an inherent part of my childhood, I was completely oblivious to the feeling. But more than anything else, it was the shame I felt, even when I didn't know it was shame, that helped me change.

TALES FROM THE MEMORY BANK

When I look back at my childhood, all I can see is constant shame. The shame of having no clean clothes and wearing the same socks and underwear for a week. The shame of not having a school uniform so I stood out from the other children, which of course didn't go unnoticed by the bullies.

The shame of not even having something as essential for a teenage girl as a sanitary towel.

Physical education at school was a real trial for me, knowing that someone would always notice me trying to hide my shame in the corner of the changing rooms. I was never invited to other children's birthday parties as they knew I wouldn't be allowed to go. That exclusion heaped more shame upon my young shoulders.

On top of all the shame I felt for the things that could have been changed if someone had just cared enough to help me, bizarrely, I felt shame for being a redhead. For some reason, everyone and their mother seemed to have an issue with the colour of my hair and the freckles that came with it. I have always been tiny, and for some, that was a no-no, too. It was almost as if people were constantly looking for reasons to shame me.

Having divorced parents was a huge stigma back then. It was virtually unheard of in my childhood to come from a broken family – we were the only one in the school. What I didn't realise then was that I was carrying far more shame than any child should have to bear.

When parents conduct themselves in a shameful way, then it is the whole family that carries the shame like a sack of rocks. Every time one or other parent acts badly, the sack gets heavier.

TALES FROM THE MEMORY BANK

The fact that my parents didn't care for or protect me, and the shame I felt because of this, actually taught me a valuable life lesson. I have always redressed the balance with my own children, ensuring they have had all the love, care and attention I was denied. Some people have said I've taken this too far, but if one of my children wanted to be by my side night and day, in my opinion, that was OK. That was my role as a mum: to love and protect my kids until they were ready to manage the journey on their own.

It certainly hasn't damaged my children in any way. They have grown up to be well balanced, educated, kind, loving individuals.

My parents' shame was passed on to me via the violent environment that I was exposed to. Are children not supposed to be more precious than anything else in life? Yet I was abandoned to suffer abuse, giving my parents space to pursue their own interests. Wow, if that's not telling a child they have no value, then what is? No wonder shame followed me wherever I went.

As if to reinforce the shame dumped upon me by my family circumstances, a courtroom judge decided my father was a suitable carer for me and my other siblings after he had been convicted of grievous bodily harm on a family member. What message does that give out, other than that I had no value in the eyes our parents, society, even the law? I knew something should be different, I knew this wasn't right, but no one was listening or cared. The shame I felt grew and grew; it became normal to experience degradation and humiliation. The message I was receiving loud and clear from the adults around me was that I deserved the shame, it was as it should be.

Carrying shame

I was forced to experience sexual acts way before I was able to manage or understand them. In later life, this led to me noticing I was more promiscuous than those around me, a realisation that brought with it shame that cut deep. I honestly didn't know this wasn't normal. What I did know was that I was forbidden to talk about any of it. This alone carries shame.

Whose shame it was that I was bearing opens up a whole new set of questions. In my case, one person's shame – my father's – had been transferred on to the other person involved – me. A little person. A child robbed of her innocence.

Until I started exploring and understanding the shame I had carried from childhood, the shame that had been thrust upon me by the people who were meant to care for me, it stuck with me. As a parent, I had no idea what was a normal level of sexual interest for a child. Was it

OK for a child to be inquisitive about the opposite sex? To my regret, I at times shamed my own children in my head. Thank goodness that I was far enough into my therapy to identify this and not pass the shame that I carried on to my kids.

TALES FROM THE MEMORY BANK

The shame of the stealing I felt forced into as a child simply so I could eat not only carried into adulthood, but also transferred to my kids. When they decided to test the water and try stealing for themselves, yes, I shamed them. I called the police and made them pay everything back.

Is that healthy shame? I believe it is. It taught them values, giving them the opportunity to make personal changes and decide who they wanted to be. This conscious shaming, I believe, helped to shape them into the people they are today.

A close friend once decided to get some materials and didn't pay, although he had intended to. This didn't feel right, and he had a very restless night afterwards; this linked straight back to his own past experience of shame and the reality that whatever we do, there are consequences.

Is it OK to have an affair and expect your children to cover for you? Is it OK to steal someone's peace of mind? Is it OK to leave those around you in fear? Is it OK to lie? Is it OK to force your opinion on another, not allowing them the freedom to grow with their own points of view? Is it OK to shame someone if they change their mind? Is it OK to abandon your children? Is it OK to force your sexual desires on to another? Is it OK for professionals to make jokes about people's mental illness? My list of shame from my past, dumped on me by others, could be endless.

Carrying shame from the past isn't always a bad thing, though. It can instigate change that needs to happen. Shame about our actions and the consequences of them, how they impact on us and those around us, can send us on a journey of learning and growth. But if we are carrying the shame of someone else's actions, we must learn to let it go. It's their shame, not ours, and we have no need to continue to burden ourselves with it.

Learning to cope with shame

I discovered an excellent book called *Healing the Shame that Binds You* by John Bradshaw.[3] I was doing my group therapy training at the time, which I was struggling with as my own inadequacies and strong beliefs born from a dysfunctional childhood weren't proving to be the best grounding. On top of that, I was surrounded by a group of people who could not see the value of personal growth in their professional growth.

---

3   J Bradshaw *Healing the Shame that Binds You* (Health Communications, 2006)

Some people doing the training were unkind about the people they were supposed to be helping. They thought nothing of gossiping about others, then having the audacity to claim they cared. This brought into question my own values. I felt the shame of being around people who said they cared, but acted in a completely different way.

Listening to John Bradshaw's book in my car on the way to training, I equipped myself with insight and started to patch together some of the experiences I had suffered throughout my life. I realised how to look into myself until I had dealt with my own shame, and separated it from the shame dumped on me by others.

Combining hope and change, for me, was tinged with the underlying feeling of worthlessness that shame brings. Recognising that, fundamentally, the shame had been brought on by others who had done nothing to own it and had therefore transferred it to me, I started to free myself from this sense of worthlessness.

If someone in the caring profession fails to explore and own their shame, the chances are they will drive it into others, usually the vulnerable people they are supposed to be helping. Having witnessed this in my work, I wonder why accountability to explore one's self isn't a prerequisite for being given the precious job of helping vulnerable people.

Shame brings with it a whole set of rules. Unless you have recognised and worked through shame and its rules, you won't know if that is the reason behind a lot of the responses you give to various situations, or where the shame has come from.

If you never ask for your own needs to be met, this can be a clear indicator that you're living with shame from the past that you need to deal with. This can manifest in a number of ways, from not making a choice for yourself from a restaurant menu, to never picking a holiday destination, or indeed deciding for yourself whether you want to go on holiday or not. The reality is that you deserve all of these choices, and more, but if those around you don't or didn't give you any empowerment, the chances are you won't give it to yourself.

This is something I'm still working on today. I can be honest with myself and recognise the shame I need to leave behind, but I struggle to ask for my desires to be met, no matter who I'm with.

TALES FROM THE MEMORY BANK

As I rarely had anything nice given to me when I was a child, and never from my parents, when I grew up, I didn't feel I had the right to ask for what I wanted. In fact, I felt shame that I wanted things, and this has been difficult to come to terms with.

Nowadays, when I'm given a gift, while I appreciate it, I feel ashamed to accept it. If I'm given something I really don't like, then I feel even more ashamed. Who am I to feel so ungrateful when someone has gone to the trouble of buying me a present? All this is thanks to poor parenting and transference of shame.

I recently experienced a similar kind of shame when sorting out the loft. I really didn't want to throw away things from my children's past. My joy at seeing their schoolwork when they were little made it feel like I was chucking out my history, which was painful. It reminded me of having my teddy bear taken away from me when I was a child. I was brokenhearted, and to this day, I remember the tears of losing my best friend, my confidant. When our children had special toys, imaginary friends, I always embraced them. But now, the attachment I had to the past, even good memories, was manifesting itself in my old fallback of shame.

Splitting

Does shame always hold back growth, or do we allow shame to hold back our growth? Big question, and one I feel I can answer. Yes, I allowed shame to hold me back. I still do to a certain degree.

For me, when I allow shame to hold back my growth, it manifests itself in good old splitting; some people call it disassociation, but splitting is my word. When I detach from a situation that is painful, it's a coping strategy that has been both helpful and unhelpful: helpful because it has allowed me to cope in some horrendous situations, but unhelpful because it cut me off from my emotions. I still do this, although now I recognise that I'm doing it. My family, friends and work colleagues also know if I'm segregating my feelings and realise that means things are not going well in my world.

I'm a forgiving person and I have found this to be helpful. If shame is crippling my growth, I have to retreat into myself – practise splitting. Then I can forgive myself so I can move on. Splitting allows me the time and space to heal. It gives me the opportunity to contemplate without causing anyone else pain. It isn't something I use often, but using it in this way has turned what could be a negative coping strategy into a useful one.

TALES FROM THE MEMORY BANK

I recently had to use my splitting strategy when I discovered someone had been lying to me for some time. I'm not someone that you need to lie to; I might not like the truth, but it is what it is. Once I know the truth, I can deal with it. If I'm being lied to, I am denied the choice to deal with the truth, and I really don't appreciate being denied choices.

I had to detach before I could go forward. This was the only way I could heal from the shame of being lied to. My scars run deep, so to have them reopened hurts and it takes time for me to move on, especially when the person causing the pain – in this case the one who had decided to lie – is someone I want in my life.

Whenever a scar from the past is reopened, I can take it one of two ways. As always, I have choices. I can act as a victim, allow the shame I felt in the past to overwhelm me again and disappear into it, which has devastating repercussions for my growth. Or I can run with it, accept it for what it is, realise I can only change myself and leave others to own the shame and responsibility for their poor decisions.

Shame will only control you if you let it, and I do my best not to allow this to happen to me. If I do allow it to take over, it just causes me more pain, and why would I want to do that to myself? Shame is like a low cloud, attaching its damp darkness to everything it envelops. It chills us, obscures our vision and destroys our clarity. Shame can feel heavy and disorienting, but with insight, we can learn to recognise its symptoms and allow ourselves to change.

Once I had figured that shame was holding me back, my course became clear. It was like opening heavy curtains and allowing sunshine into a darkened room for the first time. I recognised that I had been carrying my family's shame: the constant secrets that we had to keep, from my father's gambling addiction to the slavery and the constant abuse and violence that went with it; the shame that my mother had left me and my siblings with our father and put us at risk. None of this shame was mine, but I took it all on board. It took a long time to realise that this was what I was doing.

TALES FROM THE MEMORY BANK

Splitting to prevent the shame of the most current event that has caused me pain, whatever it may be, has allowed me to detach and cope. I also use splitting when I'm in a situation I find traumatic.

For example, I don't do blood, so I have had to detach when I am faced with a gushing wound. I then have the ability to manage the situation, and after it is all over and done with, I allow myself to examine my feelings.

When a woman with terminal illness asked me to make sure she died in a certain setting, splitting came to my rescue, as it was a difficult situation to deal with. Temporarily putting my feelings to one side helped a lot. I was able to do what she asked of me, supporting this woman in her time of desperate need.

Using shame

Having insight into shame has helped me to keep myself on track to be a good person. The horrible feeling shame brings with it, especially when it's linked to being a parent or making a judgement error that impacts on others, keeps me on my toes.

My conduct as a parent before I decided to make changes wasn't always the best. While I could allow the shame of this to pull me down, instead, I have used the insights it has given me as a useful deterrent to make sure I never go backwards. The thought of repeating those mistakes fills me with horror and inspires me to do my best.

Shame can prevent or promote growth. It can be kind and cruel all at the same time. It can encroach on our lives like the tide coming in, slowly creeping and covering the ground, getting into every crevice. It can obscure our view, but only if we let it.

Shame and the insights it has given me have allowed my growth more than any other emotion. And it hasn't run out of steam. The shame of abuse doesn't ever really disappear, but it settles. When I least expect it, sometimes it comes along and hits me over the head. The ugly shame of the past can chase me around, but being open and honest without having to expose myself too much has always helped. Expressing my feelings, without necessarily going into detail, to a great counsellor or a trusted friend strips shame of its power.

When all is said and done, shame has its good and not so good bits. It can inspire and prevent. It can remind us of who we want to be and who we don't. The reality is that some people will push their shame on to us. We need to remind ourselves that it's their shame, not ours, challenge it and have the courage to prevent it reoccurring.

NINE
Legacy

From the moment we are born, the only thing we can guarantee is that one day, we will die. Wow, that's a huge concept, isn't it? Does the thought of death bring you trepidation or acceptance?

Personally, I link thoughts of my inevitable demise to a positive: the legacy I will leave. My father's legacy has continued to cause pain to others. For me, this isn't an option. I want my family and those around me to have positive memories of me when I'm gone, so I have chosen to move on and build a good life rather than repeating the patterns of my childhood.

TALES FROM THE MEMORY BANK

A nice man I knew left his guitar to his nephew, who took his fondness for the guitar and the tunes they'd played together into his future. His children enjoy hearing him play the guitar, and in this way his uncle's legacy is carried on to the next generation.

The uncle had been a vulnerable man, tortured by mental ill health and chronic addiction. His only possessions when I knew him were a few clothes, some family photos and his guitar. He had been a well-respected musician with lots of potential, and he also taught guitar to others in recovery, but he was unable to conquer his own demons.

When I received a call to say he had passed away, I wasn't surprised, just sad and relieved all at the same time. The legacy of the beautiful tunes he played and his inherent kindness hopefully outweighed the pain caused to himself and others by his addiction.

His story serves to show that our legacy doesn't need to be something huge that everyone takes notice of. A guitar player who makes one person smile can leave a legacy that is just as worthwhile.

There are many people in our world who have a worthwhile legacy to leave, but often, we don't see them for who they are. Society has created a level of judgement, stereotyping and compartmentalising people, putting them into a kind of league table, much like we see in football. Those who have wealth and status are in the Premier League. It is these people we often aspire to emulate. Those with mental illness are in the lower leagues, struggling to survive, and those suffering from addiction are in non-league, their value unrecognised unless they happen to score a lucky goal and get spotted by a talent scout. Part of the legacy I want to leave is to be that talent scout and bring recognition to those who both need and deserve it.

The legacy of my childhood

But what of the legacy left to me? What is the long-term impact of losing my innocence at an early age, having to bypass my childhood because of adult interference? Being catapulted into adult situations before I was naturally equipped to know what is right or wrong? What is normal, what is not? One legacy is that this dilemma taunts me to this day.

If I let them, questions can plague me. Is it normal to wear that? Is it OK to wear that? What are normal and OK anyway? I didn't have a clue about bedroom toys, for example, until my daughter had an Ann Summers party. I ended up taking the catalogue home to my husband and he explained. How crazy – my daughter educating me about sex. Talk about growing into adult life in the wrong order. We laugh about it now, yet at the time I was mortified.

I am impressed by the freedom my children and their friends have to express their sexuality openly and be confident around it. It still amazes me. Thank goodness I was able to give my children a very different legacy to the one I received. At an early age, I linked sex to doing as I was told and hating every minute of it, so as an adult, I never enjoyed the natural inquisitiveness most people feel as their sexual self awakens.

A legacy of poor parenting was that I didn't know about puberty when my body started to change. I didn't have a clue then what was normal, and even when my own kids reached puberty, I had to ask as many questions of my husband as they did. We laughed about it as a family, but it brought a tear inside. The reason for my lack of knowledge, the legacy of my childhood, always meant my laughter was tinged with sadness. I had no idea about self-care. Plucking my eyebrows, for example, was an enigma to me. My mother gave me some tweezers and a mirror and told me to get on with it.

When I reached young adulthood, I didn't know that you could love someone without having to be intimate on a physical level. Nor did I realise that love could be given and received equally. No wonder I had no sexual boundaries when I was young and ended up considering myself promiscuous.

Thanks to being half starved as a child, I still have little understanding around how much food to buy and tend to fill the cupboards as if there is going to be a nuclear war. We could probably live for six months and not have to shop. No one ever goes hungry in my house. Alongside this, I love to provide for others and see family meals as a vital part of family life. Something I rarely experienced as a child was sitting together as a family at the end of the day, talking about what had happened since the morning. I insisted this happened throughout my kids' childhood, and they have replicated this in their own families. I'm saying this with a smile on my face. It's a legacy I hope the grandchildren carry on.

TALES FROM THE MEMORY BANK

I regularly challenge myself about what I eat, thinking I've eaten too much. This links to the poor body image which was established from negative messages when I was a child. I didn't show my legs for years due to being told by a boyfriend they were awful. Actually, they're not, but for a long time, I honestly thought they were.

I continually struggle with the fat card. No matter what the scales or those around me say, it's a struggle to convince myself I am not fat. I can be 7, 8 or 9 stone, and still see the same fat person that I was conditioned to see, to the point I won't wear certain clothes if my body image is having a bad day. My whole wardrobe is spread out on the bed before I decide what to wear to go out for the evening and it's a chore to put it all back when we return. My husband hates it, but just accepts it's the way I am. I can't change the legacy from my childhood.

TALES FROM THE MEMORY BANK

I would much rather be at home than on holiday. Home is my security, even though I never had that as a child. In fact, the legacy of my turbulent home life as a child is that I now feel extra safe and secure in my nice adulthood home and have such gratitude for it, I just want to be there all the time. Holidays can be a chore. Even though I have had some wonderful times, I find it hard to go and get terribly home sick.

I was never equipped with the experience of travelling when I was a child, so I made sure to redress the balance when bringing up our children. They have grown up with a good understanding of a holiday; they still reminisce about camping on Exmoor, playing in the river, building a campfire, singing, taking bike rides and enjoying amazing family time. Our grandchildren have also had the benefit of family holidays, especially when Granddad is camping in the garden.

TALES FROM THE MEMORY BANK

Illness is something I find really hard to deal with. My mother took to her bed around the age of forty and has stayed there on and off ever since. I never quite believed in her illness, as it came and went when it suited. When those around showed her sympathy, then she was sick. When there was no one around to wait on her hand and foot, she made a miraculous recovery.

I have had a serious illness for some time, but I have struggled to allow myself to be sick. I push myself to carry on when really, I should be resting. This could be seen as a positive – I never give up and give in to illness, but long term, it can be to the detriment of my health. I'm so scared of being my mother that I deny myself the right to be ill. Not a legacy I want to leave for others.

All of these legacies sit in the waiting room of my life, intruding into my reality every so often. You could ask why the hell I haven't moved on. I have; they are all things I continually work on. But they'll stay there in the background, reminding me of who I was.

They also remind me of who I can be: the best person possible under any circumstances. While I cannot change what happened to me, I can change what happens in the future. I don't force my opinion on to my children; I give them choices. My love for them is built on mutual respect. Our healthy relationship allows us all to be individuals rather than forcing them to be clones of me. Although I sometimes have to see the pain other people's actions inflict on them, the legacy of my past has given me the insight to support them, whatever the outcome.

Am I a good parent? You'll have to ask my children. While it was horrendous, my childhood taught me how a parent should never behave. Am I a good wife? I believe so, another legacy of learning what not to do at an early age. My mother was submissive and regularly allowed herself to be bullied, which is something I have worked hard not to carry into my adult life and the lives of my children.

Work ethic

A good work ethic isn't something that I consider my parents to have had. When she was younger, my mother worked extremely hard to provide herself with a good home, but in her later years, she made the decision not to work and received benefits instead. My father, to my knowledge, always worked, but he kept everything he earned to himself and never shared.

As I write this, I realise I'm probably the least selfish person I know thanks to his legacy. He would count the biscuits so he'd know if we children had had any. He would measure the level in the bottle of squash as it was all for him. We had a freezer delivered one day, full of amazing food. He ate his way through it all without batting an eyelid while his daughters stood looking on, starving hungry.

Do I have a good work ethic? Yes, I do. Perhaps it's too good sometimes, but it has given me a great career and the opportunity to help others move on from their own demons. The legacy of my parents is always going to be there inside me, but I no longer give it power. What I do is use the knowledge it's given me to change.

I consider it a privilege to work hard to help others. This opportunity has allowed me to save lives and be instrumental in people changing their destiny. It's an amazing feeling seeing others change for the better. I've seen babies being born and women becoming the mothers they want to be. I've had fathers sharing the joy of self-discovery with me.

I've challenged communities, told the truth when others were scared. I've confronted bullies and kept my principles, even when it would have been easier not to. I've instigated change, standing my ground until policies and procedures were put in place to offer support and structure.

I have pushed myself to the limits in more ways than one. I jumped out of an aeroplane even though I suffer from both vertigo and motion sickness, raising loads of money for charity. I've helped thousands of people to find their own way in life. I've met plenty of people on my journey who didn't agree with me. That doesn't make them wrong, just different, and for those differences, I'm grateful. It's about the legacy each of us wants to leave.

I can be a tough boss, but I'm an even tougher advocate. I will support my team, friends, family and anyone else who may need it, and I'm proud of this. I will stand my ground and never allow others to bully or be bullied.

Conclusion

When I die, I hope more people will say good things than bad about me. But even those who didn't like what they saw can learn from my mistakes, as I have from those who came before me.

'There but for the grace.' Throughout my life, this saying has given me hope that I can change my circumstances as well as gratitude for the things I have. Witnessing the traumas others have suffered, I am eternally grateful that I haven't had to go through the same.

There is always a silver lining. You just have to open your eyes and look for it. I'm the luckiest person in the world, even though my story may not always reflect this. I have a beautiful family, a home, friends, a career, food in my tummy and I'm warm. I was never warm as little girl, and so I realise this is a gift.

My gratitude extends to all those who have touched my life. I have had the privilege of learning from you all.

Acknowledgements

Thank you to the people who have helped me get the book this far – you know who you are. Thanks for letting me be me and choose my own path, and for not forcing me into a box.

The Author

Angie Clarke MBACP is an accredited counsellor and therapist with more than three decades' experience. She is the founder and director of Somewhere House, an addiction rehabilitation centre in Somerset. Drawing on her first-hand experiences of overcoming life's difficulties, Angie aims to inspire others and give them hope to turn their lives around. She spends her time either at home with her family, horses, dogs, cat and husband, or in her office at Somewhere House. This is her first book.

🌐 https://www.angieclarke.com

Lightning Source UK Ltd.
Milton Keynes UK
UKHW020957140622
404410UK00008B/376